# 801 THINGS YOU SHOULD KNOW

*From*

## GREEK PHILOSOPHY *to* TODAY'S TECHNOLOGY

### THEORIES, EVENTS, DISCOVERIES, TRENDS, AND MOVEMENTS THAT MATTER

## DAVID OLSEN

Avon, Massachusetts

Published by
Adams Media, a division of F+W Media, Inc.
57 Littlefield Street, Avon, MA 02322. U.S.A.
*www.adamsmedia.com*

ISBN 10: 1-4405-6571-6
ISBN 13: 978-1-4405-6571-7
eISBN 10: 1-4405-6572-4
eISBN 13: 978-1-4405-6572-4

Printed in the United States of America.

10   9   8   7   6   5   4   3   2

*This book is available at quantity discounts for bulk purchases.*

*For information, please call 1-800-289-0963.*

FOR DAD AND MOM

# CONTENTS

# INTRODUCTION

Abnegate. Confabulate. Encomium. Hyperopia. Ineluctable. Monolithic. Peripatetic. Saturnine. Torpor. Zenith.

It is hard to believe that my book *The Words You Should Know* has been in print for more than twenty years. That book has become a bestseller for a simple reason—it lays out in an easy-to-read format the "essential" vocabulary words that people need to know. Other vocabulary books contain lots of words you will never hear. *The Words You Should Know*, on the other hand, helps people quickly master the words they need to know and hear around them every day.

Aesthetics. Baroque. Class Consciousness. Existentialism. Feudalism. Fortissimo. Impressionism. Multilateralism. Sword of Damocles. Theory of Relativity.

Based on the same philosophy, in a brief authoritative style, *801 Things You Should Know* presents the leading ideas and concepts every educated person should know.

Lots of people need a quick and authoritative way to identify and define the ideas they hear around them every day, whether in the news media or in our culture in general.

If you've ever confronted one of these terms, you know that the usual approach—stalling for time until you can grasp the context of what the person has just said, or dredging through your mind for a few elusive memories from a high school or college classroom—has its limits. With a few minutes of study each day, the book's straightforward, succinct definitions will help you become the master of conversation and help you to understand what is being said around you. This book can get you out of a jam, improve your performance at school, and help advance your career. And that's no hyperbole, rigmarole, or embellishment.

In this book I have done the work of culling out essential terms and ideas. All you have to do is read through the brief descriptions of the ideas and understand them.

Each section contains 100 ideas or concepts that a person needs to know. The categories are philosophy, history, business and economics, art and literature, people and culture, politics, science and technology, and social sciences.

Someone once said that knowledge is power. To a large extent that is true. Knowing the ideas and concepts in *801 Things You Should Know* will put you in a position to advance in your career, social circles, or school. But more important, you can quickly expand your appreciation of the world around you and how it became what it is today.

So whether you are studying for the SAT or ACT, want to sound more intelligent in conversation or around the office, or wish to expand your knowledge of politics, philosophy, art, business, or science, you'll be more successful when you master this book.

But above all, I want to create that rarity among vocabulary and reference books—one you can leaf through enjoyably. Have fun!

# 1

# THINGS
## YOU SHOULD
## KNOW ABOUT
## PHILOSOPHY

66 Until philosophers are kings, or the kings and princes of this world have the spirit and power of philosophy, and political greatness and wisdom meet in one, and those commoner natures who pursue either to the exclusion of the other are compelled to stand aside, cities will never have rest from their evils—no, nor the human race, as I believe—and then only will our State have a possibility of life and behold the light of day. 99

—Plato

In this section you'll learn the 100 things you need to know about philosophy, from all of Plato's best ideas to modern-day philosophies such as subjective idealism and infinitism. You will learn how, in the age of reason in England and France, there was a reshuffling of thought and ideas central to humans and their place in society. How Confucius built an ethical system and moral order of virtues credited with instilling values of learning and family devotion that are common in China today. How humanism stresses human fulfillment through science and the application of scientifically derived knowledge. How the mind-body problem explores the question of whether a soul exists in humans or if we are a collection of chemicals that interact to provide experience of the external world. How transcendentalism teaches that reality can be discovered through intuitive thought processes, and makes a priority of spiritual insights over empirical data. You will learn all this and much, much more.

# AESTHETICS

This is the philosophy of beauty and taste relating to nature or the creation of art. It's an appreciation of beauty derived through the senses or a study of sensory-related values or judgments. It can also mean a critical review of art forms or culture. It comes from Greek, meaning "I perceive, feel, or sense."

# AGE OF REASON

In eighteenth-century England and France, philosophy, art, religion, and society's values were re-evaluated through the prism of reason. It was a time of reshuffling thoughts and ideas central to humans and our place in society. Many thinkers of this age promoted the importance of the individual in society, challenged the right of monarchs to rule, and said people should pursue their own course in life. What transpired in this period of history set the stage for democratic upheavals such as the American Revolution.

# AGNOSTICISM

A doubt or skepticism about the existence of God; beliefs or judgments about whether it is possible even to know about the existence or nonexistence of a God or deity. The term also relates to the likelihood of our knowing metaphysical or religious truths. Agnosticism includes the belief that humankind has not acquired adequate proof for a rational decision as to the existence of a deity.

# ANIMISM

The belief that animals, plants, mountains, rivers, and other natural phenomena possess a spirit. Animists argue for the existence of both the physical and spiritual worlds in one world. Ancient tribal people attributed myths and rituals to certain animals or acts of nature, giving them specific powers. Anthropologists often refer to the religious practices of ancient people as animist.

# ANTHROPOMORPHISM

The attribution of human emotions and features to animals, spirits, gods, or natural phenomena such as thunder and lightning, the sun, etc. The ancient Greeks thought of their gods in human form. Anthropomorphism can include physical appearance, temperament, and personality. Mythic gods who showed emotion, indifference, etc., are anthropomorphic gods.

# AQUINAS, THOMAS (1225–1274)

An Italian philosopher and Roman Catholic theologian who wrote the *Summa Theologiae* as a comprehensive overview of Christian belief. His work was the high point of Scholasticism, a scholarly approach to critical thinking using Aristotelian logic. In his writings, Aquinas encouraged the application of reason to theological topics.

# ARISTOTLE (384 B.C.E.–322 B.C.E.)

A Greek philosopher who as a young man was taught by Plato. Next to his teacher, Aristotle is considered one of the world's greatest philosophers. He studied and taught about almost every aspect of science, knowledge, rhetoric, logic, ethics, biology, and zoology. His approach to studying objects was later used by Francis Bacon to develop the scientific method. Aristotle was, for a time, the tutor of Alexander the Great.

# ASCETICISM

Self-denial; forgoing pleasure, daily convenience, and financial security to satisfy religious pursuits or spiritual achievements. Asceticism means denying the body through self-discipline to strengthen the spirit. Ascetics lead a simple lifestyle, restricting sensual pleasures and the enjoyment of life.

# BUDDHISM

The name is applied to religions practiced widely in India and Southeast Asia based on teachings of Siddhartha Gautama, known as Buddha, who lived between 600 B.C.E. and 400 B.C.E. The term means "the awakened one." The goal of the Buddha's teachings is nirvana, the highest level of happiness. Through his insights, people may transcend this world by accepting suffering as a means to overcome ignorance.

# CALVIN, JOHN (1509–1564)

A French theologian and one of the Protestant reformers, he taught that people are saved by God's grace and not by their individual good works. Calvin considered human beings totally depraved in their fallen state and unable to act ethically or morally. He taught that God has predestined some people for eternal damnation and others for a heavenly abode.

# CALVINISM

The belief of John Calvin, the Protestant reformer, that people are saved by God's grace and not by their individual good works. Calvin taught that humankind has limited free will and is completely dependent on God's sovereign grace. Calvin is most widely known for his doctrine of predestination, which states that God has chosen some people for eternal damnation and others for salvation. But it is God's choice as to whom he decides to save.

# CLOCKWORK UNIVERSE

Following the introduction of Isaac Newton's laws of motion in the seventeenth century, philosophers conceived of the universe as a clock wound up by God. The moving parts, or gears of the watch, were controlled by God's laws of physics. This idea gained popularity in the eighteenth-century Enlightenment because through gravitation and other natural laws, the movements of the solar system could be explained.

## CONCEPTUALISM

The medieval theory that there are no universal concepts outside our perception, unlike Plato who thought universals had an objective existence. According to this theory, people conceptualize meaning and experience and impose a structure upon it.

## CONFUCIANISM

Confucius (551 B.C.E–479 B.C.E.) taught about love of humanity, harmony between thought and conduct, and reverence for parents, including ancestor worship. He built an ethical system around these concepts, stressing moral order and virtues. His philosophical and ethical system had great influence on Chinese culture and is credited with instilling values of learning and family devotion that are common in China today. Confucianism predates the introduction of Buddhism and Daoism, which eventually became the prevailing philosophies of thought in China. But over time, many of the ideas of Buddhism and Daoism were combined with Confucianism and neo-Confucianism was born.

## CREATIONISM

The belief that all things were created as they now exist by God under his powers, which are mysterious and unknowable to man. Creationists don't believe that life forms gradually developed and evolved to bring about the earth as we know it today. Creationists believe the account of the earth's creation found in the book of Genesis in the Bible, in which God created the earth in seven days.

# DAOISM

To live in harmony with one's surroundings. This philosophical system, which developed in China, stresses the virtues of a simple life with little or no interference with the course of natural events. Taoists try to live in harmony with the Tao (Dao), a term that means the path or principle that is the driving force behind existence.

# DEDUCTIVE REASONING

Top-down logic. This means starting from a general statement to reach a conclusion that is logical and sound. Inductive reasoning is the reverse of deductive reasoning, in which conclusions are reached from the examination of specific examples.

# DEISM

A belief in God based on reason and rational thought. Deists look at the order and beauty of the world and universe and conclude that God is the designer and first cause, though he is distant and indifferent to his creation. Deists reject revelation as revealing the existence of God. The term originated in the 1620s from the French word *deisme*, which derives from the Latin *deus*, "god."

# DEONTOLOGY

In ethics, the beliefs a person holds concerning duty or moral obligation. It can also mean the determination of the morality of a choice based on the rules present in the situation.

# DESCARTES, RENÉ (1596–1650)

A philosopher and mathematician who lived in France, he is considered the father of modern philosophy. He is best known for conceiving of his ability to doubt as proof of his existence (*Cogito, ergo sum*—I think, therefore I am). As well, his ideas on dualism, that reality comprises two substances or principles that are either mental or material, have been extremely influential. He is also credited with founding the science of analytic geometry.

# DETERMINISM

The view that natural laws determine facts and events, that human choices and events are caused by some force or law.

# DOGMA

The doctrines or teaching of an institution. The Catholic doctrine of papal infallibility is an example of Catholic dogma. It is an established opinion that members of a church share and that unites the group. The word comes from Latin, meaning "philosophical tenet," and Greek, "that which one thinks is true."

# DUALISM

In philosophy, the idea that reality comprises two substances or principles, which are either mental or material. Monism, on the other hand, is the belief that there is one basic principle or substance that comprises reality, while pluralism is the belief that there are several substances or principles upon which reality is founded. In theology, it is the belief that there are two forces such as good and evil, and that people have two parts, soul and body.

# ECUMENISM

Efforts to promote Christian unity worldwide. There has been, since the 1800s among Protestant groups, an international movement to unite Christian churches and denominations across the globe. Some churches oppose ecumenical efforts because they are reluctant to compromise on their doctrines.

# EGOISM

Viewing things exclusively from your own perspective and vantage point and not seeing things from others' perspectives; the belief that your own best interest is the highest good. In ethics, egoism means that morality is achieved through self-interest. In psychology, egocentrism is a preoccupation with your inner world.

# EMPIRICISM

The idea that knowledge comes solely from your sense data—what you see, hear, feel, and therefore know. Empiricism is about knowing through experience and observation.

# EPICUREANISM

The belief that the highest good is pleasure, but not in a hedonistic manner. Epicureans devote themselves to sensual pleasures and the enjoyment of life through modest living, knowledge of the world, and experience. Epicurus taught that existence has come about from blind chance and that the pursuit of pleasure is the highest aim of life.

# EPISTEMOLOGY

How you know things; the nature of knowledge and understanding; the study and theory of the methods of acquiring knowledge. The term is related to truth, belief, and justification. It was first formally named by James Ferrier (1808–1864) in the nineteenth century.

## ETHICAL RELATIVISM

The idea that what is right and wrong depends on the situation and there are no absolute ethics. In this system, the views and values of the individual determine what is ethical, based upon the situations of culture and history. Ethical relativism has been debated since the time of the earliest Greek philosophers.

## EXISTENTIALISM

A philosophical movement in the twentieth century. An existentialist believes that individuals are responsible for the authenticity of their choices. They determine their own place in reality in a universe that is meaningless. Thus people are entirely free and have a responsibility to make themselves. With this realization and this newfound responsibility come despair and dread, but they vanish once a person has made himself or herself through this newfound freedom.

## FATALISM

The acceptance of fate; a belief that all events are and were inevitable or predetermined and that we are powerless to change our destiny. Thus we do not need to assert ourselves because we have no power over the future. A more nuanced view suggests that people are powerless to do anything other than what they actually do.

## FINITISM

The idea that the only things that can be put into mathematical concepts are finite. A mathematical object does not exist unless it can be derived from natural numbers.

# FREE WILL

Contrary to determinism or fatalism, this concept argues that individuals are free to make choices, think, and act voluntarily. A personal choice is made by *you* and is not influenced by outside factors.

# HEDONISM

The pursuit of an individual's pleasure and happiness are the highest aims of life. Hedonists engage in sensual pleasures to the maximum degree, believing that an individual should experience more pleasure than pain and discomfort in life. Modern-day hedonistic philosopher Michel Onfray (1959–) defines hedonism "as an introspective attitude to life based on taking pleasure yourself and pleasuring others, without harming yourself or anyone else."

# HEGEL, GEORG (1770–1831)

German philosopher who proposed an absolute idealism, in which a person's intellect is the highest expression of what is true and absolute. Hegel argued the human mind is able to perceive the world around it and resolve the contradictions into an integrated whole.

# HERODOTUS (484 B.C.E.–425 B.C.E.)

The father of history, Herodotus was the first author to record a narrative history of events. He chronicled events of the Persian invasion of Greece between 490 B.C.E. and 479 B.C.E. in his book *The Histories*.

# HINDUISM

The dominant religion of India. However, there are many different schools of belief within Hinduism. Brahma is the supreme god, but the religion includes the worship of many deities. Hindus are born into a caste system, which determines social status and various human rights. The religion also supports the belief that after death a person's soul is born into another body as the soul strives for perfection. Hinduism teaches that a soul should seek freedom from the material world by eliminating personal desires and purifying oneself.

# HOBBES, THOMAS (1588–1679)

An English political philosopher, he is best known for his book *Leviathan* in which he espouses his views on absolute sovereignty and the rights of the individual in society. He taught that political power is best served when it is representative of the consent of the people.

# HUMANISM

People should use reason to understand the natural world and man's place in it. There is a focus on human fulfillment through science and the application of scientifically derived knowledge along with the belief that humans should act on reasoned judgment to advance the cause of humanity. Humanism discourages a belief in a supreme being, arguing instead that there is no power superior to humanity and the purpose of life is to advance the happiness of humankind through intellectual pursuits.

# HUME, DAVID (1711–1776)

Scottish philosopher who specialized in empiricism and skepticism. He believed that the only reliable knowledge comes through the senses.

# IDEALISM

In a philosophical sense, the notion that things can have an ideal form, apart from how we perceive them. Idealists believe that ideas and concepts are the foundations of reality and govern our experience of the world. What we perceive as reality is mentally constructed or immaterial. This branch of philosophy was influential throughout nineteenth-century philosophy, particularly with Immanuel Kant and Georg Hegel.

# INFINITISM

The idea that knowledge may be contained in an infinite chain of knowledge and based on the concept of infinity or infinite realism. The founder of infinitism, Jean-Pierre Fenyo, said, "The most important thought is Infinity! And one who understands that has the ability to understand the philosophy of infinitism."

# JAMES, WILLIAM (1842–1910)

An American philosopher and psychologist, he was a pragmatic, espousing the idea of practicality as a means for discovering truth and meaning. James argued that to discover the true content of an idea, you must first dissect it and discover the idea's practical applicability.

# KANT, IMMANUEL (1724–1804)

In his work, the *Critique of Pure Reason*, this German thinker attempted to merge the principles of reason and truth derived through sense experience. Kant was an idealist and believed that objects and concepts have an ideal form.

## KIERKEGAARD, SØREN (1813–1855)

Although a theologian, Kierkegaard, a Dane, was critical of organized Christian churches. He was among the founders of existentialism and believed that an individual is responsible for the authenticity of his or her choices.

## LOCKE, JOHN (1632–1704)

An English philosopher, he is regarded as one of the leading thinkers of the Enlightenment. Famous for his social contract theory that explained the rights of the individual citizen and government, his ideas were very influential in the American and French revolutions.

## LOGIC

Making correct inferences from data or evidence. Logic is the method by which reason is achieved or knowledge is gathered. Deductive reasoning is the "logical" process by which a conclusion follows a premise and is supported with facts, so the conclusion must be true based on the evidence presented. Also related to logic is inductive reasoning, whereby a conclusion is supported by various premises.

## MACHIAVELLI, NICCOLÒ (1469–1527)

He is most famous for his book, *The Prince*, written about his native Italy. In the book he argues that a prince must be ruthless and cunning to be successful. The ideas in *The Prince* were controversial in their day because they clashed with prevailing political thought. Today the book is regarded as the first work of modern political philosophy.

## MATERIALISM

A system of thought arguing that matter, energy, and the laws of motion make up the universe. To a philosophical materialist, matter is the only reality. She believes that mind, or emotion and thoughts, are the function of only physical interactions and rejects anything supernatural.

## METAPHYSICS

The branch of philosophy dealing with being and knowing. Metaphysics concerns itself with such subjects as the great first causes of things, the reality of God as the principal creator of the world, and the meaning inherent in the existence of humans, the stars, and the universe. The term comes from the Greek philosopher Aristotle's work on the subjects of the first principles of ontology (the study of being) and epistemology (the study of knowledge).

## MILL, JOHN STUART (1773–1836)

Mill, an English philosopher, was the originator of utilitarianism, believing that moral choices and actions lead to the greatest good for the greatest number of people. He wrote that actions should be judged as right or wrong based on the good they produce.

## MIND-BODY PROBLEM

The relationship between the mind as a conscious, perceiving entity and the physical structure of the brain. In philosophy, the term refers to the relationship between mind and matter. Those who study this problem investigate whether a human has a soul or whether he or she is a collection of chemicals that interact to provide the experience of the external world.

# MONISM

The notion that there is one principle or basic substance that comprises reality; the reduction of all things to a single idea or governing principle. By extension, monism suggests the idea that there is one cause for all things coming into existence.

# MONOTHEISM

The belief in a single supreme being. The term can also refer to a oneness with God. Polytheism and pantheism refer to a belief system comprising many gods, as in Greek and Roman mythology or Hinduism. The term comes from the Greek word *monos,* meaning "single," and the Greek word *theos,* meaning "God."

# MONTESQUIEU, CHARLES (1689–1755)

A French philosopher who influenced political thought during the Enlightenment in Europe. He is credited with the idea of separation of powers within the government, such as appears in the U.S. Constitution. His ideas are included in many of the modern-day constitutions.

# MORALITY

Your ability to make choices about your conduct or that of others according to rules of rightness; to pursue the good and virtuous in life. An amoral person lives without moral judgments.

## MYSTICISM

Pertaining to knowledge of the mysteries that surpass everyday knowledge and are only known to those initiated into a restricted group; the belief that spiritual and cosmic truths can be revealed to human beings through meditations and trance-like states. The Greek word *mystical* refers to secret religious ritual, while *mystikos* refers to an initiate of a mystery religion—for example, the worship of the Greek god Dionysius.

## NATURAL LAW

Universal laws, originating in nature, as the fundamental principles of existence; propositions that should guide human behavior and action because of their universal truth and application. Natural law is discovered, according to its adherents, by observing the natural world and using reason rather than revelation from a spiritual source. In philosophy, natural law is the idea that society should be governed by natural principles of existence deduced from reason.

## NATURALISM

The idea that the natural world comprises natural elements and forces of motion; a deterministic view of life that natural laws determine facts and events. Naturalism says that human choices and events are caused by some force or scientific law or are determined. There is no place for spiritual ideas and revelation from an otherworldly source.

## NIETZSCHE, FRIEDRICH (1844–1900)

A German philosopher, he was known for his strong criticism of Christianity, which he believed was a means to control and subdue the people. He espoused his view that the Superman was a driving force for progress through history and that it is a good thing that in the world certain people of high intelligence, ingenuity, and drive will rise to the top of society to rule over others.

# NIHILISM

Life is inherently meaningless except for what meaning people carve out of their lives as part of their existence. Political institutions, religions, social mores, and laws are constructed to impose meaning and structure on a meaningless world. In the nineteenth century, nihilists emerged as political radicals, intent on overthrowing the rulers of society.

# OCKHAM, WILLIAM OF (1228–1348)

An English philosopher and Franciscan friar, he is considered one of the thought leaders of the fourteenth century. He was known as a Scholastic philosopher but is most famous for Ockham's razor, a proposition that in essence states that the simplest solution is usually the best.

# ONTOLOGICAL ARGUMENT

An argument for the existence of God. The argument goes as follows: God is a being; there is nothing greater than God. We can conceive of such a being. A being that existed in both mind and reality would be greater than one only existing in the mind. We can conceive of such a being. Therefore, God must exist. In the seventeenth century, philosopher René Descartes proposed a similar argument: the idea of God's existence is determined from the idea of a supreme perfect being that can exist.

# ONTOLOGY

The study of human existence or being; speculation on the nature of reality and what it means to exist. Ontology is one of the three main areas of study for philosophy, the other two being epistemology and ethics.

# PACIFISM

A viewpoint opposed to war or military action. A pacifist refuses to serve in the military in a fighting capacity because it is contradictory to his or her beliefs. Pacifism supports the idea that conflicts between nations should be settled without war of any kind.

# PANTHEISM

Emphasis on God as an ethereal part of nature and the moving force behind nature. Pantheists believe that God is the ultimate reality and that the universe, humans, and nature are manifestations of God's transcendence. Pantheism comes from Greek and means belief that "everything is God." Though sometimes confused, pantheism and atheism are quite different. Atheism holds there is no God, while pantheism holds that God is in everything.

# PASCAL, BLAISE (1623–1662)

This French philosopher was also a mathematician and scientist who made discoveries in atmospheric pressure and hydraulics. After a religious experience, he abandoned science and concentrated his efforts on theology and philosophy. He's known for Pascal's wager: You lose nothing by believing in God and living a good life, in the hope of an eternal reward; but if you reject God, and he exists, you are condemned to eternal damnation.

# PERFECTIBILITY OF MAN

A man may achieve perfection in his lifetime through his own self-discipline and effort. God's influence or grace is not part of that process. This idea was made popular by the French philosopher Jean-Jacques Rousseau (1712–1778), who wrote extensively on the progress of mankind from brute savages to men and women of refinement. He wrote: "All the subsequent progress has been in appearance so many steps toward the perfection of the individual."

# PLATO (427 B.C.E.–347 B.C.E.)

A Greek philosopher, widely believed to be the most influential Western thinker of all time. He taught that objects have universal forms and meanings outside of the senses that exist in another realm, thus becoming the founder of idealism. He was taught by Socrates and later himself taught Aristotle. His most widely read works are *The Republic* and *Symposium*.

## PLATONISM

Ideas derived from the philosopher Plato; in particular, the notion that abstract objects exist independently in reality apart from what we perceive through the senses or understand intellectually. Platonism also argues that mathematical concepts really exist and are independent of human thought. For example, Plato would say that abstract numbers ("2") exist independently of their physical manifestation ("2 chairs," "2 people," etc.).

## PLURALISM

In philosophy, the idea that there is more than one substance or principle that makes up reality. Dualism is the idea that reality comprises two substances or principles that are either mental or material. Monism is the belief that there is one basic principle or substance that comprises reality. In politics, the word "pluralism" is sometimes applied to a situation in which several independent groups compete for and/or share power for the right to govern.

## POLYTHEISM

Belief in many gods. The ancient Greeks and Romans were polytheistic. Monotheism, on the other hand, is the belief in one supreme God.

## POSITIVISM

The idea that when trying to reach conclusions about the first causes of the universe, positive facts and evidence should take precedence over speculation. Positivists reject metaphysics and religious speculation and believe that we should only collect data empirically. Logical positivism is a method of critically analyzing only data and phenomena that are verifiable.

## PRAGMATISM

In philosophy, the idea of practicality as a means for discovering truth and meaning. Philosophic pragmatists look at the practical consequences of a thing rather than engaging in abstract theorizing.

## *THE PRINCE*

Famous book by philosopher Niccolò Machiavelli published in 1532. Widely read since its publication for its teachings on strategies for political or financial gain. Machiavelli believed that a king or lord should employ cunning and ruthlessness to gain power and, once gained, hold on to it. An Italian diplomat and historian, he was heavily involved in the politics of his native state of Florence. *The Prince* is credited as one of the first works of political philosophy.

## RATIONALISM

Applying the principles of reason as the foundation for the search for truth; the belief that in matters of opinion, a rational approach will determine truth. Rationalists claim the human mind is not prewired with a set of concepts relating to truth. Reason alone is the best path to knowledge and surpasses even experience, as the human mind can be deceived into believing what it is experiencing is truthful. There is no place for divine revelation in rationalism because reason cannot be applied to the supernatural.

# REALISM

A medieval school of thought that argued for the existence of Universals in the world. These Universals, the realists argued, are measureable and objective or real.

# REID, THOMAS (1710–1796)

Scottish philosopher. Reid did not agree with philosophers who taught that a person's perceptions and biases are all they can know about the world. He instead believed that our common sense tells us about the reality of the external world and that knowledge can create a foundation to build on.

# RELATIVISM

Based on the person or culture, a decision may be right or wrong; things are relative to the situation and circumstances. Truth is not absolute—rather, the conception of truth may vary from situation to situation. A person's opinion or point of view has no absolute truth but reflects his or her life experiences and biases.

# RHETORIC

The art of employing language to make effective arguments; effective use of language and words to present a case; to persuade or influence through proper use of language and ideas. Rhetoric may have a negative connotation, implying speech without substance.

## ROUSSEAU, JEAN-JACQUES (1712–1778)

A French philosopher whose writings and thought significantly influenced the eighteenth-century French Revolution, as well as modern conceptions of political freedom and social change. Rousseau described a person's need for a comprehensive education as a path to ideal citizenship. His sentimental fictional writings introduced the early styles of romanticism. An eclectic man, Rousseau also composed music and operas. He was interred in the French Pantheon in Paris for his many contributions to French art, music, and politics.

## RUGGED INDIVIDUALISM

The belief that an individual should be free from constraints of personal liberty and has the ability in a free society to create himself or herself. Individualism includes the belief that people can make it on their own without government assistance based on their own talents and abilities.

## RUSSELL, BERTRAND (1872–1970)

British philosopher, one of the first analytic thinkers who put mathematical logic at the center of philosophy. Russell was also a pacifist and involved in many political causes throughout his life.

## SARTRE, JEAN-PAUL (1905–1980)

French philosopher who was a leading existentialist. Sartre was widely known for his philosophical writings, his plays, his left-leaning political views, and his long relationship with the writer and philosopher Simone de Beauvoir (1908–1986).

## SKEPTICISM

Questioning the possibility that a certain truth or thing can exist. Skeptics argue that a proposition should not be believed if it cannot be proved through the techniques of reason.

## SOCRATES (469 B.C.E.–399 B.C.E.)

Greek philosopher, teacher of Plato, who is one of two sources for Socrates' teachings. Socrates employed the Socratic method of teaching: posing questions and challenging students to review their preconceptions. He taught that virtue leads to knowledge. In 399 B.C.E. he was condemned to death by the citizens of Athens on charges that he was corrupting the youth. He calmly accepted his fate and drank poison.

## SOLIPSISM

The belief that you can only be certain of the existence of your own mind. Solipsism is skeptical of other people's ideas and perceptions of reality. Instead, this belief holds that what you as an individual experience and know is more truthful and of higher value than what other people claim to experience and know. The term "solipsism" is sometimes also applied to a person who is self-absorbed.

## SOPHISTS

Ancient Greek philosophers who taught rhetoric, disputation, and politics. They were known to be less interested in the logical soundness of ideas than in their skill in presenting them. Plato accused them of desiring to win arguments simply by using clever tactics rather than pursuing truth. Today a sophist is one who uses faulty logic and rhetorically successful tactics to win arguments or make points with style over substance.

# SPINOZA, BENEDICT DE (1632–1677)

A Dutch rationalist philosopher. He argued that the human mind is not prewired with a set of concepts relating to truth. Reason alone is the best path to knowledge and surpasses even experience, as the human mind can be deceived into believing what it perceives is truthful.

# ST. AUGUSTINE (354–430)

A prominent theologian in the early Roman Catholic Church. His writings and teachings, particularly *City of God*, helped to shape Roman Catholic doctrine. He is credited with writing about God's nature as "a circle whose center was everywhere and its circumference nowhere."

# STOICISM

In philosophy, the idea that one should maintain a reasoned approach to emotion and an indifference to pain or pleasure. This path will lead to wisdom and happiness. Stoics argued that unchecked emotions lead to errors in reason. They linked their philosophy to an idea of cosmic determinism: People were free to act but should align their lives and choices with the principles of the universe, which in turn would lead to the most wisdom and happiness.

# SUBJECTIVE IDEALISM

The doctrine that the world does not exist outside a person's ideas or sensations. All human experience exists solely in the human mind. Material things have no existence outside our perceptions of them.

## SUPERMAN

A concept developed by philosopher Friedrich Nietzsche (1844–1900). The Superman asserts his or her will to dominate others. Nietzsche believed it a good thing that certain people of high intelligence, ingenuity, and drive rise to the top of society to rule over others. The Superman thus represents the ideal of human evolution and has overcome the struggle between Good and Evil.

## TABULA RASA

Latin for "blank slate." People are born into the world impressionable, with no previous dispositions. A person is shaped or molded entirely based upon the types of experiences she undergoes. The term also refers to a thing in its undefiled or original state—for instance, John Locke's idea of a mind in its unformed infant state.

## TAOISM

Chinese philosophy that mandates a simple life, going with the flow of natural events, living in harmony with the Tao—that is, the path of life or the way of the universe. People can achieve happiness by not interfering with natural events and accepting what happens.

## TRANSCENDENTALISM

The idea that reality can be discovered through intuitive thought processes and spiritual insights, rather than through gathering observable data. The transcendentalists searched for answers to questions by divine appeal to God or spiritualism. They encouraged people to observe the world around them as a smaller model of the larger universe. This philosophy is closely associated with Ralph Waldo Emerson (1803–1882) and Henry David Thoreau (1817–1862).

# UTILITARIANISM

The philosophy that moral choices and actions are those that lead to the greatest good for the greatest number of people. Based on the concept of utility, it argues that action and progress should promote the greatest amount of health and prosperity for a society. The philosopher John Stuart Mill (1806–1873) wrote extensively on the concept of utilitarianism.

# VOLTAIRE (1694–1778)

French philosopher and a prominent figure in the French Enlightenment. He was a forthright spokesperson for political and religious liberties and was occasionally banished from France for his opinions. Besides being a philosopher, he also conducted scientific studies and wrote poems and plays, as well as the novel *Candide*.

# YIN AND YANG

A Chinese concept that two forces, yin (passive, feminine, dark, and negative) and yang (active, masculine, light, and positive), interact to influence all things in the universe. The two forces balance each other to produce harmony. Enlightened people sense the yin and yang forces about them in the world in the political turn of events or in nature in the change of the season.

# ZEN

A moment of enlightenment for a student seeking truth. A person who seeks Zen meditates on his or her essential nature. However, Zen encourages all means and paths to enlightenment, whether through educational pursuits or life experiences. Zen originated in China in the sixth century and appeared in Japan in the twelfth century.

# THINGS
## YOU SHOULD
## KNOW ABOUT
# HISTORY

" A small body of determined spirits fired by an unquenchable faith in their mission can alter the course of history. "

— Mohandas Gandhi

In this section you'll learn the 100 things you need to know about history, from the ancient world and its mythologies through modern times and the progress of mankind. You will learn how Attila the Hun was nicknamed the "Scourge of God." How in the eleventh century the Vikings settled in areas of Great Britain where they had previously plundered. How the belief in the divine right of kings in Europe meant that monarchs received their authority to rule directly from God and therefore could not be challenged. How in the French Revolution King Louis XVI and Queen Marie Antoinette were tried for treason and executed at the guillotine. How Manifest Destiny convinced Americans that their country was destined to expand throughout North America. All this and lots of other interesting stuff is covered in this chapter.

# ABOLITIONISM

A movement in eighteenth- and nineteenth-century America to abolish slavery among African Americans. The movement also had echoes abroad: British territories ended the slave trade in 1807 and Great Britain abolished it in 1833. In the United States, President Abraham Lincoln's Emancipation Proclamation in 1865 freed the slaves. However, before the Civil War many citizens in the North favored ending slavery immediately without compensation to the slave owners.

# ALEXANDER THE GREAT (356 B.C.E.–323 B.C.E.)

King of Macedon and ruler of much of the known world, he was famous for conquering the ancient world to the boundaries of India. He established the city of Alexandria and conquered the Persian Empire, Egypt, and extended Greece's rule throughout Asia into India. Legend has it that Alexander wept because there were no more nations to conquer. He died at thirty-two.

# ALIEN AND SEDITION ACTS

Near the end of the eighteenth century, these acts were passed by Congress and signed into law by U.S. president John Adams (1735–1826) in order to curb the activities of radicals who criticized his federalist ideas and supported the French Revolution. Many people opposed Adams's plans to increase the size and scope of the federal government and instead supported the right of states to determine policy for their citizens.

# *THE AMERICAN CRISIS*

"These are the times that try men's souls." *The American Crisis* was a series of pamphlets written and published by Thomas Paine during the American Revolutionary War. Paine wrote about the need for revolution and the right of humans to secure their freedom.

## ANTEBELLUM ERA

Period from 1781 to 1860, ending just prior to the U.S. Civil War. The term refers to society and culture in the Southern states during that time. The South had risen to great economic prominence in the antebellum era due to the expansion of slave-based cotton production after the invention of the cotton gin. After losing the Civil War, the Southern states suffered under Reconstruction, during which their culture and economic powers dwindled.

## ARTICLES OF CONFEDERATION

This document, agreed to by the thirteen American colonies in 1777, set up the first American nation as a confederacy. The Articles of Confederation put agreements in place that called for a weak federal system, with strong powers for the individual states. There were no federal executive or judicial branches of government. The legislature under the Articles of Confederation had few powers and could not collect taxes. The articles were replaced in 1789 by the stronger, more centralized U.S. Constitution.

## ATHENS

The Greek capital and the political power center of the ancient world; the most powerful city in the fifth century B.C.E. Athens became known for its sophisticated culture and philosophy and as the birthplace of democracy. Much of Western civilization as it is known today came from Greece, and in particular from fifth-century Athens.

## ATTILA THE HUN (?–453)

In the fifth century, the ruthless king of the Huns. This Asiatic tribe was feared for cruelty, murder, and torture. Attila led his armies through central and eastern Europe, and successfully invaded the Roman Empire in 452. The Romans responded by naming him the "Scourge of God."

## AUGUSTUS CAESAR (63 B.C.E.– C.E. 14)

Known as a reformer of Roman culture and politics, the first Roman emperor, born Octavius, ruled from 27 B.C.E. to C.E. 14 He achieved power after defeating his enemy Marcus Antonius at the end of a period of civil war following the assassination of Julius Caesar in 44 B.C.E. A promoter of the Roman arts, he presided over a period of peace for the empire. Because of this, as well as Augustus's devotion to history and poetry, his reign is considered the golden age of Roman literature. The term "Caesar" became attached to the office of supreme Roman ruler.

## BABYLON

An ancient and powerful city on the Euphrates River in southwest Asia. The city was at its height of power between 2800 B.C.E. and 1750 B.C.E. and was known the world over for its wealth, culture, and depravity. The Hanging Gardens of Babylon—gardens planted on terraces in the city—were among the Seven Wonders of the Ancient World. Babylon has become a symbol for anything that is wicked and corrupt.

## BASTILLE

The fortress prison built in the fourteenth century in Paris, France, made infamous on account of its cruelty to prisoners and its deplorable conditions. Here, the French government held and tortured political prisoners in the period leading up to the French Revolution. Revolutionaries attacked the Bastille in 1789 and released the prisoners; ironically, at the time, only seven prisoners remained. The attack on the Bastille often marks the beginning of the French Revolution, and Bastille Day is celebrated as a national holiday in France.

## BILL OF RIGHTS

The first ten amendments to the U.S. Constitution, mandating such rights as freedom of speech, freedom of the press, and the right to assembly. More generally, the term means any document outlining a guarantee of civil rights. The English Bill of Rights was created in 1689 and is called the Declaration of Rights. It outlines the liberties and rights of the subjects to the king and queen.

## BLACK DEATH

In the fourteenth century the bubonic plague, called the Black Death, spread through Asia and Europe. Believed to have started in Asia, it ended the lives of between 25 percent and 33 percent of the population of Western Europe, or nearly 50 million people. Fleas carried by rodents transmitted the disease; a more virulent form, pneumonic plague, was airborne. Symptoms before death included fever and painful swelling in the groin and armpits.

## BOLSHEVIKS

In Russia prior to the revolution that ushered in Soviet rule, members of the left wing of the Social Democratic Party who fought for takeover of power by the workers. Instead of peaceful or gradual political change in Russia, they called for violent overthrow of the Provisional Government, which had come to power in February 1917. Led by Vladimir Lenin (1870–1924), the Bolsheviks were radical Marxists; after the revolution of October 1917, their faction changed its name to the Communist Party of the Soviet Union.

## BREAD AND CIRCUSES

In ancient Rome, entertainment provided for the masses to divert attention from the nation's struggling economy and other national problems in order to prevent an uprising. As Roman civilization teetered on the brink of collapse, politicians said to provide the people with bread and circuses so they will ignore the signs of trouble. Today, governments use similar measures to reduce popular discontent.

## BRITISH EMPIRE

Under the British crown, starting in the eighteenth century, the vast control of countries and colonies around the globe by the British. At one point, people said that the sun never set on the British Empire. The empire reached its height in the first decades of the twentieth century, ruling more than 25 percent of the population of the globe. Many of the subject countries gained their independence later in the century, though some remained part of the British Commonwealth.

## BRONZE AGE

Approximately 4500 B.C.E. to 1200 B.C.E. Following the Stone Age, the Bronze Age was characterized by the use of copper and bronze to make weapons and tools. It was followed by the Iron Age (1200 B.C.E.– C.E. 500) with the introduction of more complex and sophisticated ways of shaping metals.

## BRUTUS, MARCUS JUNIUS (85 B.C.E.–42 B.C.E.)

Roman statesman involved in the assassination of Julius Caesar in 44 B.C.E. Brutus is the lead character in Shakespeare's play *Julius Caesar*. Caesar, when stabbed by his former friend Brutus, is said to have uttered, "*Et tu Brute?*" (Even you, Brutus?). Brutus committed suicide after he was defeated in battle by Octavius (later Caesar Augustus) and Marcus Antonius. "Brutus" is now applied to someone who has betrayed.

## BYZANTINE EMPIRE

The empire that arose from the eastern half of the Roman Empire. In 476 after the fall of the Western empire, the Byzantine Empire became the dominant cultural and political legacy of Rome. The Byzantine Empire lasted until 1453, when the capital, Constantinople, fell to Turkish forces. Until the eleventh century, the empire played an important role in European politics.

## CENTRAL POWERS

In World War I, the alliance of the European countries including the German Empire, Austro-Hungarian Empire, Ottoman Empire, and the Kingdom of Bulgaria. These countries were opposed in the war by France and the United Kingdom in Western Europe, the Russian Empire in the east, and the United States.

## CHARLEMAGNE (742–814)

"Charles the Great," crowned Holy Roman Emperor in the year 800. Charlemagne's empire included modern France and Germany, as well as parts of Italy. He was a proponent of education, enacted changes in church policy and judicial reforms, and also encouraged the spread of agriculture. Because of the advances he advocated, Charlemagne was considered a model for other medieval rulers.

## *COMMON SENSE*

A pamphlet written in 1776 by Thomas Paine (1737–1809) that urged people in the American colonies to declare independence from England. The pamphlet was widely read and turned public opinion in favor of independence and support of the Revolutionary War. Prior to its publication many people were undecided about the movement for independence. The way that Paine laid out the arguments helped people understand the rationale for freedom from British rule. Paine signed the pamphlet, "Written by an Englishman."

## COMMONWEALTH

The union of a group of nation-states to further the individual interests and good of all of them. The first commonwealth was established in Britain, Scotland, and Ireland in the year 1649 when King Charles I (1600–1649) was executed during the English Civil War. A commonwealth was created in Australia when the colonies formed a union in 1901 and a constitution was signed that divided power between a federal governing body and the states. Puerto Rico, a territory of the United States of America, is also a commonwealth.

## *THE COMMUNIST MANIFESTO*

An 1848 pamphlet written by Karl Marx (1818–1883) and Friedrich Engels (1820–1895) that is credited as the foundation of Communism. Known as the world's most politically influential pamphlet, it outlined the history and present-day effects of class struggle between workers and capitalists, described the failures of capitalism and the defects in that economic system, and predicted communism's future rise to prominence on the world stage.

## CONFEDERACY

An alliance of states. Its best-known example is the alliance of the Southern states in America, formed after the South seceded from the Union in 1861. A confederacy may be an alliance or union of governments, groups, or individuals who unite behind a common purpose.

## CONQUISTADORS

From the fifteenth to the seventeenth centuries, explorers and military forces of Spain and Portugal that sailed to the Americas to establish trade routes and colonize many areas. The explorers are called conquistadors since they conquered the native peoples of Mexico and Peru. The two most famous were Hernán Cortés (1485–1587) and Francisco Pizarro (1471?–1541).

## CONSTANTINOPLE

Capital of the Byzantine Empire. In 476, after the fall of the western Roman Empire, the Byzantine Empire became the dominant Roman territory; it included eastern Europe and western Asia. The Byzantine Empire lasted until 1453, the year Constantinople fell when it was attacked by Turkish forces. From this point on, Constantinople was known as Istanbul and became a Muslim city.

## COSSACKS

An elite group of horsemen from the Ukraine region of southern Russia, who flourished in the sixteenth and seventeenth centuries, though their descendants are still around today. The Cossacks were warriors who provided the Russian Empire with soldiers and spies. They were known for their horsemanship, as well as for their dances with fast music and difficult leaps. *Cossack* is a Turkic word for "adventurer."

## COUNTER-REFORMATION

In the sixteenth century, in response to the Protestant Reformation, the Roman Catholic Church launched its own reform movement to answer the claims of the Protestants. Jesuits led much of this movement that was intended both to shore up the beliefs of members of the Catholic Church and to refute the theological claims of the Protestants.

## CRUSADES

From the eleventh through the thirteenth centuries, Christians in Western Europe launched a series of military expeditions to Jerusalem to reclaim the Holy Land from the Muslim occupiers. The crusaders took over Jerusalem in 1099 but could not control the Holy Land; they were driven out of Jerusalem in the latter part of the thirteenth century. Today the term "crusade" is applied to any strong movement for or against a cause.

## CUBAN REVOLUTION

The revolution in Cuba lasted from 1956 to 1959. It ended with the overthrow of a corrupt dictatorship led by Fulgencio Batista (1901–1973) at the hands of a populist movement led by Fidel Castro (1926–) and his guerrilla fighters. Castro later became a Communist, and Cuba today is under Communist rule.

## CULTURAL REVOLUTION

A political movement in China during the 1960s. Led by a faction of the Communist government of China, the revolutionaries overhauled much of the country's education and university systems and purged much of its art, music, and literature. The actions were taken by the Red Guard, with the goal of building Chinese nationalism and loyalty to Chairman Mao Zedong (1893–1976). Also known as China's Great Proletarian Cultural Revolution.

## DARK AGES

A period in Western Europe from 500 to 1000, also known as the Early Middle Ages. Prior to this, Rome had been the main stabilizing force of the Western world. The fall of the empire meant a long cultural decline in Western Europe, marked by few freedoms for the people and tight rule by monarchs and over-lords. This period of history ended with the Renaissance of the twelfth century and the founding of the universities.

## DE-STALINIZATION

In the late 1950s, the movement to erase the influence of the Soviet leader Joseph Stalin (1878–1953) from Communist countries, especially the Soviet Union. This effort took the form of renaming cities, monuments, etc., as well as eliminating some policies instituted under Stalin who was known as a bru-tal dictator, having ordered the torture and execution of millions of his own people. His successor, Nikita Khrushchev (1894–1971), formulated and led the de-Stalinization movement.

## DIVINE RIGHT OF KINGS

The belief in Europe throughout the seventeenth century that monarchs re-ceived their authority to rule directly from God and therefore the king could not be challenged. The state labeled rebellion against the king's wishes as a sin against God. The oppressive nature of monarchies based on this principle led reformers throughout Europe to suggest the right of humans to govern themselves. These suggestions led to democratic reforms and the belief that the consent of the people should determine who leads them.

## *DRED SCOTT* DECISION

In the United States in 1857, Dred Scott (1795–1858), a black slave, sued for his freedom, claiming that he should be declared free because he had lived in free states and territories with his master. The case went to the U.S. Supreme Court, but the Court ruled against Scott on the grounds that as a slave he was not a U.S. citizen and thus had no standing to sue.

## EDWARDIAN PERIOD

Referring to the early part of the twentieth century, when Edward VII (1841–1910) was king of England. His time as king was marked by its show of wealth and privilege among the powerful and rich in England. However, his lackadaisical attitude and failure of leadership are blamed for England's lack of preparedness as the world fell into turmoil prior to World War I.

## ELIZABETHAN PERIOD

England's golden age of wealth and prosperity. Queen Elizabeth's (1533–1603) reign from 1558 through 1603. This period was marked by England's expansion abroad and cultural flourishing at home. The British navy gained superiority over the Spanish Armada in 1588, eliminating the most serious military challenge to the realm. There was new music, literature, and poetry. The Protestant Reformation brought new ideas of religious freedom and the individuality and innate gifts of human beings.

# EMANCIPATION PROCLAMATION

U.S. President Abraham Lincoln's proclamation of January 1, 1863, that freed the slaves. Lincoln issued the proclamation while the Civil War was in progress, attempting to create chaos among the Southern states and their slaves as well as strengthen support for the Union abroad. In reality, the proclamation did not immediately free any slaves because the South, or rebellious territories, did not honor it. The proclamation did not apply to the slave states of Missouri, Maryland, Kentucky, and Delaware, which stayed part of the United States. Slaves in these states were freed after the war's end.

# ENLIGHTENMENT

A philosophic movement in the seventeenth and eighteenth centuries focused on the idea that through reason humans could discern the true path to better politics, religion, and social institutions. This movement brought forth new ideas in science and religion and was the impetus for new concepts of governmental systems that enlarged political freedom. The term also has religious connotations. In Buddhism, enlightenment means to awake to new truth and to become free from the requirement to pass through more reincarnations. In Hinduism, enlightenment occurs when a person has progressed in knowledge and light to where she has a divine experience with Vishnu, a Hindu God.

# FALL OF ROME

In the fifth century, the great Roman Empire came to an end. The actual invasion that marked its fall came at the hands of the Vandals as they attacked and plundered the city. Before that time Roman civilization had been declining due to corruption of its political, economic, and social institutions. Most scholars believe the decline was slow, lasting several centuries. The last Roman emperor was Romulus Augustulus (460–500?) who abdicated his throne in the year 476.

# FERDINAND AND ISABELLA (1452–1516) (1451–1504)

Spanish monarchs in the late fifteenth century who financed the exploration of the New World. They backed Christopher Columbus's (1451–1506) expedition as he searched for a new trade route to India, but instead discovered America. Also, in the year 1492 Ferdinand and Isabella conquered the Kingdom of Granada and forced the Jews, Moors, and Muslims to convert to Christianity or leave Spain. Together, they united the different regions of Spain.

# FEUDALISM

A political and economic system prevalent in the eighth and ninth centuries in Western Europe in which a family is allowed to farm and live on a piece of land in return for providing service, usually military, to the master or lord of the region. Under feudalism, property belonged to the king, who provided large sections of land to his nobles. A vassal was the person who lived on the land and paid homage to the lord. In return for homage, the lords of the land would provide protection for the vassals. Japan and Egypt also had forms of feudalism.

# FINAL SOLUTION

A Nazi program in World War II for exterminating all European Jews. Prior to implementing the Final Solution, the Nazis had killed about 1 million Jews. In 1942, Adolf Hitler (1889–1945) created what he termed the "Final Solution of the Jewish Question." Under the direction of Hitler's deputy Heinrich Himmler (ca.1900–1945), the extermination camps were built to carry out mass slaughter of the Jews.

# FIRST AMENDMENT

The amendment to the U.S. Constitution that prohibits Congress from interfering with freedom of speech, freedom of assembly, freedom of the press, or freedom of religion. The First Amendment is the first article of the Bill of Rights. These freedoms were radical departures from the freedoms granted other people prior to the American Revolution.

## FOUR FREEDOMS

In a speech given by U.S. president Franklin D. Roosevelt (1882–1945) in January 1941 to build support for democracies around the world, he enumerated four freedoms worth fighting for: freedom of speech, freedom of worship, freedom from want, and freedom from fear. Especially after the Japanese attack on Pearl Harbor in December 1941, Roosevelt positioned the war as a struggle for freedom.

## FRENCH RESISTANCE

Small groups of people who fought against the Nazis in occupied France during World War II, using propaganda and guerrilla tactics. These groups worked together in secretive cells and published an underground newspaper to keep informed of the advances the Resistance was making to protect the country and stifle the efforts of the Germans. The groups provided intelligence to the official French army and ran escape networks to help soldiers get back to Allied territory.

## FRENCH REVOLUTION

A ten-year revolution in France starting in 1789. In the first phase, the revolution ended the rule of the Capet monarchy and the French aristocracy; the conflict ended with Napoleon's victory in 1799. The legislative assembly declared itself the voice of the people, and King Louis XVI (1754–1793) and Queen Marie Antoinette (1755–1793) were tried for treason and executed at the guillotine. Government passed to a group of radicals, the Jacobins, and the Reign of Terror began. Thousands of nobles and others considered enemies to the state were executed.

## GENGHIS KHAN (ca. 1162–1227)

Mongolian conqueror whose empire reached from the Pacific Ocean to the Black Sea. His conquests included much of northern China and southwest Asia. He was greatly feared for his barbaric cruelty, the rape of women and children, and the ruthless slaughter of all who stood in his path.

## GETTYSBURG ADDRESS

U.S. President Abraham Lincoln's speech, delivered November 19, 1863, to dedicate the national cemetery at the Civil War battlefield in Gettysburg, Pennsylvania. "Fourscore and seven years ago our fathers brought forth on this continent a new nation, conceived in Liberty and dedicated to the proposition that all men are created equal." Lincoln's speech was only three minutes long but many consider it among the most important documents of American history.

## GLORIOUS REVOLUTION

A revolution in England in 1688 during which King James II (1633–1701) was forced by the British parliament to abdicate the throne. In his place, Mary II (1662–1694) and William III (1650–1702) were installed as co-monarchs. The cause of the upheaval was largely James II's attempt to declare his royal prerogative over Parliament. The event is also called the "bloodless revolution," although there were battles in Scotland and Ireland. As a condition of ascending to the throne, Mary II, daughter of James II, and her husband, William III, agreed to create a Bill of Rights.

## GUTENBERG, JOHANNES (ca.1395–1468)

He was the first printer to use movable type and a press to print books and pamphlets. Considered one of the most influential inventions of all time, his movable type and press enabled books to be widely distributed and allowed the flow of new ideas. Gutenberg played a major role in bringing to pass the age of the Renaissance and the scientific revolution, as well as the Protestant Reformation.

## HOLY ROMAN EMPIRE

Empire established in central Europe when Charlemagne (742–814) was crowned Roman emperor in 800; a loose confederation of regions in Europe ruled by the laws and customs of the ancient Roman Empire. It was governed by a German king who was referred to as the Roman emperor. For its existence, the emperors were of German or Austrian descent. The empire declined in power from the sixteenth century and ended in 1806 when the Roman king Francis II (1768–1835) abdicated the title.

## HOMESTEAD ACT

In 1862 this law made western lands in the United States available to settlers at no payment. The intention of the Homestead Act was to encourage westward migration, so provisions granted settlers with farmland divided into 160-acre sections. The homesteaders were required to cultivate the land or build a residence on it, as well as live on it for five years.

## A HOUSE DIVIDED

An 1858 speech by Abraham Lincoln at the Republican Party convention. Lincoln referenced "a house divided against itself cannot stand," found in the book of Matthew, to emphasize the danger arising from the unresolved slavery issue between the North and the South. Lincoln warned that "I do not expect the house to fall—but I do expect it will cease to be divided. It will become all one thing, or all the other."

## HUNDRED YEARS' WAR

A series of conflicts between England and France that occurred between 1337 and 1453 over English possessions in France. Since the year 1066 when William the Conqueror (ca. 1028–1087) became the king of England, English kings had been required to pay homage to the French king. In 1337 the English king, Edward III (1312–1377), refused. The French sought to seize Edward's lands in France, while Edward declared that he was the rightful king of France.

## HUNS

A nomadic tribe that dominated parts of central and eastern Europe in the fifth century. In World War I and World War II, the Germans were referred to derogatorily as Huns.

## INDUSTRIAL REVOLUTION

In the eighteenth century, the shift from hand tools in farming and manufacturing to powered tools and machines. Industrialization began in England and spread rapidly to other countries. The main source of power was the steam engine, which dramatically increased factory output and productivity, creating wealth for the factory owners. The transition to manufacturing also caused a population shift as people left their farms to work in factories in the cities.

## INQUISITION

Investigations held by the Roman Catholic Church to discover and punish heresy. In many cases the accused were tortured to obtain a confession. If found guilty, a person could be excommunicated and turned over to the local government authorities for execution. The first inquisitions were held in France and then spread to other European countries. Today, when a person is questioned severely about a matter, they're said to undergo an inquisition.

## IRON AGE

Period following the Bronze Age, lasting roughly from 1200 B.C.E. to C.E. 500. The Iron Age was marked by advanced techniques of shaping metals to make weapons and tools in Europe, Africa, and Asia. The use of iron increased because it was more plentiful than bronze, although iron was a somewhat less durable metal.

## JACKSONIAN DEMOCRACY

With the beginning of the presidency of Andrew Jackson (1767–1845) in 1830, the movement to give more power and greater rights to the average citizen gathered force. Jacksonian democracy was opposed to providing special privileges to the wealthy and powerful. The ideas supporting the Jacksonian movement were first articulated in the southern and western settlements of the United States. Eventually, the movement led to an extension of the right to vote to white males throughout the country.

## JEFFERSONIAN DEMOCRACY

Movement led by U.S. President Thomas Jefferson (1743–1826) to extend more rights and privileges to the people through democratic reforms. Jefferson believed the people would elect the men best suited for leadership of the country. The supporters of Jefferson believed that governance belonged to the farmer and average everyday citizen and distrusted the aristocracy. Jacksonian democracy took this concept further, espousing the view that the common people could decide for themselves what was best on national and state issues.

## JOAN OF ARC (ca. 1412–1431)

In the fifteenth century, a seventeen-year-old French girl led the army of the French dauphin, later Charles VII (1403–1461), during the Hundred Years' War. She believed that God spoke to her to help her obtain victory, which permitted the dauphin to be crowned as the rightful French king. After being captured by the Burgundians and sold to the English, she was burned at the stake for heresy.

## JULIUS CAESAR (100 B.C.E.–44 B.C.E.)

Roman general and statesman who conquered Gaul and Britain for Rome. By today's standards, he would be considered a populist politician, appealing to the masses with clever rhetoric and emphasizing his status as a successful general to gain their favor.

## KOREAN WAR

War between North Korea and South Korea from 1950 to 1953. The United States and other countries belonging to the United Nations supported South Korea. Communist China supported North Korea. It was as much a war of ideologies between free democracy and Communism as a conflict between the two countries. The fighting ended in a truce in 1953.

## LABOR MOVEMENT

A movement beginning in the eighteenth century to secure better wages and working conditions for laborers. By joining forces in an organization, workers had more bargaining power to negotiate. The early history of the labor movement is filled with tension and even violence as workers and their representatives fought long battles with many of the manufacturing facilities, railroads, oil production companies, etc.

## LADY GODIVA

According to legend, in the eleventh century Lady Godiva, a noblewoman, rode naked through the streets of Coventry in England to protest the high taxes imposed by her husband. The term "peeping Tom" is believed to have originated from this same legend; a man named Tom was struck blind for not turning his eyes away from the naked woman.

## LEAGUE OF NATIONS

Created by the Treaty of Versailles after World War I to promote world peace and provide a platform for unity among the nations. Countries belonging to the League of Nations worked together to solve problems with refugees and immigration, improve health conditions, prevent disease, etc. The United States never joined the League of Nations because the U.S. Senate refused to ratify the league's covenant. The League of Nations was disbanded in 1946 to make way for the creation of the United Nations.

## LONG MARCH

In 1934, the Communist Chinese Red Army retreated to northwestern China after being driven out of southeastern China by Chiang Kai-shek (1887–1975) and his army. During the march Mao Zedong became the Communist Party leader. About 100,000 men started the journey and only 8,000 finished the trek. In the northeast, Mao Zedong and his army fought Japanese invaders and Chinese government troops while gradually renewing their strength.

## LOST GENERATION

The men and women who returned home from World War I disillusioned by their war experience, wondering what they had sacrificed for. Many believed they had fought to protect the older, failing institutions of their fathers. They also felt lost in the societal changes brought to pass by the war. Ernest Hemingway (1899–1961) and F. Scott Fitzgerald (1896–1940) were notable writers whose works reflect the disillusionment they experienced.

## LUDDITES

In nineteenth-century England, groups of workers vandalized manufacturing equipment to protest the loss of jobs the machines represented. They also organized riots outside English factories. Most Luddites were textile workers, the dominant industry in England. Today a Luddite is anyone hostile to new technology or change.

## MAGELLAN, FERDINAND (ca. 1480–1521)

Portuguese explorer who circumnavigated the world and discovered the Straits of Magellan in 1520. These straits, near the southern tip of South America, are the connecting point of the Pacific and Atlantic oceans. Magellan is also credited with discovering the Philippines, though he was murdered there by a native.

## MAGINOT LINE

Prior to World War II, fortifications built along France's eastern border to keep the Germans from invading France. The French thought the Maginot Line was impenetrable, but learned their mistake when the German troops simply went around the line in the north and spilled into France in 1940.

## MAGNA CARTA

In 1215 in England, barons forced King John (1166–1216) to sign a charter of English rights and liberties. This document required the king to recognize the rights of the barons, church, and citizenry. The monarch could not take away property without a trial or increase taxes without permission of Parliament. The term sometimes refers to a country's founding constitution that outlines rights and liberties.

## MANIFEST DESTINY

In the early nineteenth century, the belief that the United States was destined to expand and control all of North America. According to this idea, God desired American ideals of freedom and capitalism to be spread throughout the continent. This belief both caused and was spurred on by the vast migration west as well as provided the justification for annexing the southwest parts of the continent.

## MESOPOTAMIA

Known as the cradle of civilization, this ancient area in western Asia is now part of Iraq. It is the site of several ancient civilizations including the Assyrian, Sumerian, and Hittite. People in Mesopotamia living between the Tigris and Euphrates rivers were among the first to achieve an agricultural surplus and to invent a written language.

## MIDDLE AGES

Roughly, from 500 to 1500 in Western Europe. The Middle Ages cover the period from the end of the old world, which had known Roman rule for many centuries, to the beginning of the Renaissance in Italy.

# NAZISM

In Germany, the movement led by the National Socialist German Workers' Party. In 1933, Adolf Hitler took control of the organization. The Nazis believed that Germans were part of a master Aryan race. To maintain the purity of the race, the Nazis sought to exterminate not only the Jews but also people with physical or mental handicaps. To find *lebensraum* or "living space" for the German people, the German government sought to take over Europe and rule under a thousand-year reich.

# NEW DEAL

In the twentieth century in the United States, the program of President Franklin D. Roosevelt to help America recover from the Great Depression. The New Deal called for government programs to provide work for the millions of unemployed through the Works Progress Administration, as well as the creation of programs such as Social Security to which all taxpayers would contribute but only the neediest would use as a safety net.

# NEW FRONTIER

Catchphrase developed by the administration of President John F. Kennedy to get U.S. citizens to support the space program and other initiatives of the White House. In the 1960s Americans felt as if there were no new challenges. Kennedy said there were always new opportunities, new frontiers to explore.

# NEW WORLD

The yet-to-be-explored and -conquered parts of North and South America in the fifteenth century. After Christopher Columbus discovered the Americas, explorers and military expeditions from Spain and Portugal sailed to the Americas for exploitation and conquest. They colonized many areas and were eventually joined by the British and French.

## NONVIOLENT RESISTANCE

To withstand authority in a peaceful way. Also called civil disobedience. In the United States during the 1960s, nonviolent resistance was used to fight discrimination and segregation against African Americans. Such resistance included sit-ins, marches, and Freedom Rides.

## NORMAN CONQUEST

In 1066, the Normans conquered England. Led by William the Conqueror, they sailed from Normandy to Hastings on the south coast of England, where they defeated an Anglo-Saxon army and William declared himself as king. He brought French culture and influence to England, and he established new systems of laws and administration throughout the country.

## OCTOBER REVOLUTION

Also called the Russian Revolution. In February 1917, the Russian monarchy fell and a temporary government was established. The October Revolution refers to the overthrow of the Provisional Government by the Bolsheviks and marks the start of Communist rule in the new Soviet Union. The revolution actually occurred on November 7, 1917, but the Russian calendar was, at the time, behind that used in the West.

## OTTOMAN EMPIRE

Turkish empire founded in 1300 and spread across parts of Europe, Asia, and Africa. It lasted until its collapse after World War I. In the sixteenth century, the Ottomans achieved their greatest amount of territorial control. After World War I, what remained of the Ottoman Empire became part of modern-day Turkey.

## PERSIAN EMPIRE

In ancient times, a south Asian empire established in the sixth century B.C.E. that reached from Europe to India. Alexander the Great conquered the empire in the fourth century B.C.E. At one time or another, the Persian Empire was conquered by Turks, Mongols, Greeks, and Arabs. Today, Iran is located in the heart of the ancient Persian Empire.

## PHOENICIA

An ancient seaside kingdom, which existed between 1200 B.C.E. and 1000 B.C.E. along the Mediterranean coast. Its inhabitants were traders and sailors traveling across the ancient world. The Phoenicians created an alphabet, which the Greeks and Romans adapted and which is the basis of the modern English alphabet. Today, Israel and Lebanon are located near the site of this ancient kingdom.

## POMPEII

In 79, Pompeii, a city in southwestern Italy, was buried in volcanic ash and pumice as Mount Vesuvius erupted. The city had a reputation in its day for wealth and immorality. A great deal of work, beginning in 1748, has been done to excavate the remains, which are preserved in the hardened ash and reveal a rich history of daily life.

## RECONSTRUCTION

From 1865 to 1877, after the end of the U.S. Civil War, the war-torn South rebuilt and reorganized cities, homes, and farms. The South was divided into districts under military oversight and elections were held to establish new state governments. The people of the South deeply resented being kept out of the reconstruction of their states, which was presided over by Republican politicians from the North. Carpetbaggers from the North profited from the destitute people of the South until 1877 when the last of the U.S. troops left.

# RED SCARE

The Red Scare of 1919–1920 was the result of fears that the United States might be infiltrated by the same revolutionaries responsible for the Russian Revolution. During those years, the U.S. government deported hundreds of immigrants for suspected Communist-leaning political opinions. A second Red Scare occurred in the 1950s, led by Sen. Joseph McCarthy (1908–1957).

# REFORMATION

In the sixteenth century in Europe, a religious movement that broke theologically from the teachings of the Roman Catholic Church. Also called the Protestant Reformation, it brought new ideas about religious freedom and human individuality and innate gifts. The Roman Catholic Church launched the Counter-Reformation to refute the claims of the Protestants.

# REIGN OF TERROR

During the French Revolution, many people were executed by the ruling party, the Jacobins. Between 1793 and 1794, thousands of people were sent to the guillotine on charges of treason. Maximilien de Robespierre (1758–1794) led the effort to identify people who were threats to the security of the French state in an effort to eliminate any and all areas of resistance to Jacobin rule.

# RENAISSANCE

From the fifteenth through the seventeenth centuries, Europe experienced a rebirth or renaissance of learning, art, and literature. This era marked the transition point from the Middle Ages into the modern world and led to the scientific revolution of the seventeenth century and to the period known as the Enlightenment in the eighteenth century.

# ROMAN EMPIRE

From about 27 B.C.E. through C.E. 476, the Roman Empire ruled the civilized world. The earliest origins of the city of Rome can be traced back to just prior to 753 B.C.E. However, it was in 27 B.C.E. that the Roman Empire may be said to have been formally established when Octavius Caesar was granted the title of Augustus. "All roads lead to Rome" summed up the vast land holdings and conquests of the empire. The Roman Empire was also known for its impressive aqueducts and cities of hundreds of thousands of people. Because of political corruption and invaders, the western Roman Empire weakened and collapsed in the fifth century. Its eastern remnant, the Byzantine Empire, lasted until 1453 when it fell to the Ottoman Turks.

# ROSETTA STONE

In 1799 a stone slab was found near Rosetta, Egypt, which provided the key to translating ancient Egyptian hieroglyphics. The stone displayed an inscription written in three parallel languages: Greek, demotic, and Egyptian hieroglyphics. Jean-François Champollion deciphered the Rosetta stone in 1822, and it is now in the British Museum. The term "Rosetta stone" now refers to a clue leading to the solution of a problem.

# SEVEN WONDERS OF THE ANCIENT WORLD

Of the Seven Wonders, only the Great Pyramids at Giza still exist. The other wonders included the Hanging Gardens of Babylon, the Colossus of Rhodes, the Lighthouse of Alexandria, the Temple of Artemis at Ephesus, the Statue of Zeus at Olympia, and the Mausoleum at Halicarnassus.

## STONE AGE

The period in which humankind used stone for weapons and crude tools. It preceded the Bronze Age and may have lasted several million years, ending around 4500 B.C.E. The Bronze Age was characterized by shaping metals such as bronze to make weapons and tools. The Iron Age followed the Bronze Age with the introduction of more complex and sophisticated ways of shaping metals.

## VATICAN II

The nickname for the Second Vatican Council, which met in Rome from 1962–1965 under the leadership of Pope John XXIII. It initiated a series of modernizing reforms in the church, including permission to celebrate the mass in the vernacular as well as in Latin; affirming the centrality of Scripture in the Church; and opening the Church to the outside world.

## VICTORIAN PERIOD

In the latter half of the nineteenth century, the cultural norm in Great Britain. In those days, with Queen Victoria on the throne, Great Britain was the most powerful nation in the world. The English believed, given their many colonies around the globe and the industrialization of the country, that their country was blessed by God for its righteousness.

## VIKINGS

From the eighth through the tenth century, people from Scandinavia sailed the coasts of Europe plundering and pillaging towns and settlements. The Vikings included Swedes, Danes, and Norwegians and ranged as far as Russia, where they raided Kiev and were known as Russe because of their red hair. The Vikings later settled in northern areas of Great Britain. The Viking ships, with their high sterns and bows, have become symbolic of a destructive force.

## WARS OF THE ROSES

Between 1455 and 1485, a series of sporadic wars for the English throne between the House of Lancaster, symbolized by a red rose, and the House of York, symbolized by a white rose. The wars ended at the Battle of Bosworth when Henry Tudor (1457–1509) claimed the throne after defeating the last Yorkist, King Richard III (1452–1485). Henry married Richard's niece, Elizabeth of York (1456–1503), to shore up his claim to the throne.

## WOMEN'S SUFFRAGE

The movement in the late nineteenth and early twentieth centuries to gain women the right to vote and hold office. In America the struggle started in 1848 with the Seneca Falls Convention at which Elizabeth Cady Stanton (1815–1902), Lucretia Mott (1793–1880), and others launched a campaign for the vote. Though subject to brutal attacks, both in the press and physical, the movement triumphed in 1920 with the passage of the Nineteenth Amendment to the Constitution.

# THINGS
## YOU SHOULD
## KNOW ABOUT
# BUSINESS &
# ECONOMICS

**"** Most of the important things in the world have been accomplished by people who have kept on trying when there seemed to be no hope at all. **"**

—Dale Carnegie

In this section you'll learn the 100 things you need to know about business and economics, from bear markets to insider trading to microeconomics and macroeconomics. You will learn how the balance of payments arises from a country's imports of goods and services. How limited liability corporations avoid legal exposure in the case of lawsuits. How monetarists attempt to control inflation by limiting the growth of a nation's money supply. How the higher the rate of productivity a company can deliver, the more products or services it can produce. How the purpose of Treasury bills is to help the government raise money in the short term. All this and many other valuable things can be found in this chapter.

## ACT OF GOD

In contract law, an Act of God is a clause that protects both parties from events that are naturally caused; damage resulting from earthquakes, floods, hurricanes, tornadoes, etc. It also applies if one party is prevented from carrying out a clause of the contract due to circumstances that care or experience cannot reasonably prevent.

## AGRIBUSINESS

Corporations and businesses associated with the growth, processing, and production of food from corporate farms. Agribusiness is about corporate farming and producing food on a mass scale rather than small family farms. Agribusiness employs the latest science and technology to increase crop yields and food nutrition.

## AMERICAN STOCK EXCHANGE

This was, until recently, the second-largest stock exchange in New York City. However, in 1998 it merged with the NASD exchange to become the NASDAQ. The NASDAQ is a computerized trading system.

## AMORTIZATION

To eliminate or liquidate a debt by making monthly payments to a creditor; to finance with installment payments or to write off the cost of an asset over time. The term derives from the Old French *amortir*, which means "to reduce to the point of death."

# APPROPRIATE

To authorize the use of funds for a specific purpose. For example, state legislatures often appropriate money for school districts. It can also mean to take funds without permission or authorization. For example, Bernard Madoff (1938–) appropriated his clients' money and put it in his own bank account. Derived from the Latin *appropriates*, which means "to make one's own."

# ARTICLES OF INCORPORATION

Documents that each state requires for the establishment of a business within its borders. These articles set forth the basic structure of the type of business, listing the corporate officers, the purpose of business, etc., and are kept on file as public records.

# BALANCE OF PAYMENTS

Over time, the difference between a country's payments to foreign countries and payments received from foreign countries arising from imports and exports of goods and services, including movements of cash, capital, gold, investments, tourist spending, and other resources. When a country's payments out are larger than payments received, the country suffers from an unfavorable balance of payments. The imbalance can impact the value of the country's currency in other countries.

# BALANCE OF TRADE

A country's difference in the monetary values of exports and imports. A country has a favorable balance of trade if exports are greater than imports (trade surplus), and unfavorable if the reverse is true (trade deficit).

# BALANCE SHEET

In accounting, a statement that adds up assets and credits against debts and expenses; also called a statement of financial position. Such a sheet demonstrates the financial health of a business. The balance sheet's three parts are assets, liabilities, and ownership equity.

# BANKRUPTCY

A legal status entered into when a company does not have the funds to pay its debts. Bankruptcies are overseen by a court, which determines which creditors should be paid from existing funds and which assets can be liquidated. Often, under different chapters of bankruptcy, companies are able to continue operating, and a judge determines the best course for the company until it can regain its status as a solvent company.

# BEAR MARKETS

A market in which prices are falling; the opposite of a bull market in which prices are rising. When market prices are falling, investors feel pessimistic about possible returns and are reluctant to purchase new or additional stocks. A price decline of 20 percent or more over at least a two-month period is characterized as a bear market.

# BENEFICIARY

A person or group that receives a payout of benefits (although the payout can take the form of profits or other advantages). In a will, insurance policy, or trust, the person designated as the recipient of the payout is the beneficiary. Beneficiary can also mean a person who receives funds from a government welfare program such as Social Security.

## BIG THREE, THE

The big three automakers in the United States: General Motors, Ford, and Chrysler. The largest car companies in the country and the world. The "big three" dominated the U.S. car and truck markets for decades until Japanese imports, Honda and Toyota, in the 1980s started to take away market share with more fuel-efficient and higher-quality automobiles.

## BILATERALISM

Economic or political relations between two sovereign states, including trade agreements, treaties, etc. Unilateralism or multilateralism is diplomacy by a single state or multiple states, respectively. When nations formally recognize each other, they agree to enter into diplomatic relations with ambassadors, secretaries, and undersecretaries to move along negotiations.

## BLACK MARKET

An underground market in which products and services prohibited from sale in the open market are bought and sold. In the United States, during Prohibition, a black market for illegal liquor sprang up to meet the public's demand for alcohol. Black markets do not have government oversight and often are corrupt.

## BLUE-CHIP STOCKS

Stock of an industry-leading company that has the reputation for providing quality products and good economic returns on its shares. Such stocks are sometimes listed on the Dow Jones Industrial Average, the average of thirty blue-chip stocks. These equities were originally named after blue poker chips because blue was the highest-valued chip.

## BOARD OF DIRECTORS

The directing body of a company. The chief officers of the company are members of the board and are elected by it. They are responsible for overall management and direction of the company but not the day-to-day operations. The board routinely meets and votes on a variety of issues.

## BOND

A security with a fixed rate of return that can be purchased as an investment. A bond has a date on which it will mature and can be redeemed for payment. Bonds are issued by local, state, and federal governments to raise money for projects—mostly, but not always infrastructure. Bonds can be issued by the state or federal treasuries, by city governments (municipal bonds), or private corporations.

## BOTTLENECK

When goods and services cannot get to customers due to a variety of factors, the economy is said to suffer from a bottleneck, which slows the flow of money. Similarly, a bottleneck occurs when a company is unable to grow because it does not receive the resources it needs for production because of slow growth in other sectors of the economy.

## BOTTOM LINE

Line of a financial statement showing net profit or loss. The final financial figure that appears on the bottom line of the page. The term can also mean the final outcome or crucial factor in a situation. ("The bottom line for this company is if we win this next contract.")

# BULL MARKET

A market in which prices are rising. It is the opposite of a bear market in which prices and investor confidence is falling. When market prices are rising, investors feel optimistic about possible returns and are more likely to purchase new or additional stock. A country's economic recovery, as businesses start to grow and introduce innovative products and services, can produce a bull market.

# BUSINESS CYCLE

An interval of time in a business of high and low sales, depressions, and expansions due to economic conditions; changes in business activity from booms to downturns to booms; routine business fluctuations based on economic factors.

# BUYER'S MARKET

A market where supplies of products and services exceed the demands for those products and services. In this case, manufacturers and service providers lower their prices to create incentive for the buyers. A buyer's market is considered a microeconomic trend that determines pricing in a competitive market. Ultimately, supply and demand determine how much buyers are willing to pay.

# CAPITAL EXPENDITURE

Purchase made for such things as new machines, buildings, or property for expansion; the acquisition of fixed assets for a business. Capital expenditures are made in order to build the productivity and usefulness of a business.

# CAPITAL GAIN

Economic gain, or profit, from the sale of assets, stocks, bonds, or real estate; the amount by which the selling price of the asset exceeds its cost. In general, Republicans have pushed for low capital-gain taxes to stimulate economic investment. Democrats have pushed for higher capital-gains taxes in order to counteract income inequality.

## CAPITALISM

An economic system in which private citizens own and control business and the means of production and distribution of goods. At the other end of the spectrum is Communism where the government owns and controls the means of production and natural resources. Proponents of capitalism point to innovations that better the lives of people and have been introduced into the marketplace because of the incentive to innovate.

## CAPTAINS OF INDUSTRY

A term that refers to individuals and business leaders of great renown and power. The term is reminiscent of business titans from the late nineteenth and early twentieth centuries such as John D. Rockefeller (1839–1937), Andrew Carnegie (1835–1919), and Andrew W. Mellon (1855–1937), who built large companies from the ground up and launched new productive industries. Today, the term often applies to someone who has created a large company.

## CAVEAT EMPTOR

Latin for "let the buyer beware." Unless a warranty is provided by the seller of a product, the buyer assumes risk in purchasing and using the product. In other words, the buyer should be cautious of the claims made by the seller.

## CLOSED SHOP

A business that only employs union members; a factory or manufacturing facility where union membership is required to work. To hire workers in a closed shop, the company will provide a way for them to join the union. However, right-to-work laws in some states make closed shops illegal.

## COLLATERAL

When obtaining a business loan, collateral is required to back the loan in case of default. Collateral can include physical assets such as the deed to a building as well as investments of stocks and bonds. The term also means security that a loan will be paid in full.

## COLLECTIVE BARGAINING

Negotiations between union representatives and an employer over salaries or wages, hours, and working conditions. The union represents all workers, saving the company from negotiation with each individual worker. Unions may enter into negotiations with multiple companies that need the skill set of those particular workers.

## COMMON LAW

Originally in England, the civil law based on customs and administered through the courts. Common law is a body of court decisions that are referred to as judges determine subsequent cases. This is different from statute law, which is a law passed by a legislature. Common law is the general application of the law, based on local and regional customs. After the Revolutionary War, the Americans based their court system on England's common law system.

## COMMUNISM

A social and economic system in which the state administers all property for the common good. In theory, the property and resources are owned by the community. In Communist states such as the Soviet Union, it was common for a black market or underground market to operate in the shadows. The long-term goal of a Communist government is a classless society where all things are held in common and shared among the people.

## CONFLICT OF INTEREST

A situation in which someone's action or decision will unfairly benefit him—for example, a judge's ruling that positively impacts a company in which he owns stock. When a government official or politician has business dealings in which he stands to profit from legislation he helps pass, he is said to have a conflict of interest. To avoid this, politicians can place their businesses and investments in a blind trust over which they have no control.

## CONSUMERISM

Movement to push for legislation or actions that will benefit or help protect consumers; attempts to protect consumers from fraud or dangerous products, unfair pricing, and misleading advertising. In another sense, consumerism is the idea of a growing consumption of consumer goods by a country, which is good for its economic growth.

## CREDIT RATING

Analysis of credit risks of a person, company, or country. Factors considered by the credit-rating agency include financial holdings, loan history, prior payment history including late or partial payments, and reasons why debts were incurred. A poor credit rating indicates risk and will limit the individual's, company's, or country's ability to borrow money. A sovereign credit rating for a country is a comprehensive measure of the level of risk for investors in the business of that country.

## DEBTOR NATION

A country that has borrowed more money than it is owed by other countries; a country that is behind in both principal and interest payment. Countries can owe money to other foreign countries or international financial institutions such as the World Bank. Debtor nations usually have a negative balance of trade, consuming more imports than they are exporting.

## DEFICIT FINANCING

Also called deficit spending; when a government borrows money, over and beyond what it has taken in through taxation, to spend on programs. When a government's budget exceeds tax revenues, it is forced to borrow the additional money, which usually comes from foreign governments. This creates a budget deficit. Some governments intentionally borrow money and create spending programs to help stimulate economic activity.

## DEFLATION

A drop in the general price level of an economy accompanied by an increase in the value of money in that economy. Over time this allows consumers to purchase more products and services. This is the opposite of inflation where there is a rise in the general price level of products and services as a result of too much new money being introduced into the economy. Deflation is not disinflation, which is a slowdown in the rate of inflation.

## DEPRECIATION

Decrease in the value of a product. Revaluations are made each year by municipal governments, for instance, to determine the new values for property taxes and other tax purposes. If the price of a house has declined, its value has depreciated. In accounting, the term applies when fixed assets owned by businesses lose value over time through day-to-day use. The depreciation is deducted from profits and shown as a loss for the business.

## DESPOTISM

When a despot rules a country's people and natural resources with absolute authority; tyrannical government rule, usually by one person who surrounds himself with a powerful army.

## DEVALUATION

When a country reduces the value of its money supply. A country can devalue its money in relation to another country's money supply or in relation to gold. In contrast, when a country's money supply has depreciated, it is not the result of the government's intentional action. Depreciation is the result of market forces and a weakening economy.

## ECONOMIC INDICATORS

Key statistics demonstrating the performance of a country's economy. Economists analyze this data to determine how an economy is performing. Economic indicators include a measure of inflation, unemployment, amount of imports/exports, the consumer price index, gross national product, and more.

## EMINENT DOMAIN

Government's ability to take ownership of private property for public use; court-enforced takeover of property, accompanied by fair market value payment to the owner, who can be an individual, municipality, or corporation. Most commonly, the property is used for civic purposes or economic development, including government buildings, roads, and highways.

## *E PLURIBUS UNUM*

Latin for "out of many, one." The phrase refers to the union formed by each state of the United States of America. This is the motto of the United States and is found on the coinage and seal of the United States.

## EQUILIBRIUM

Balance achieved from the influence, force, or efforts of two or more opposing forces. In economics, the circumstance in which there is neither excess demand nor excess supply in the market. In other words, when products and services balance out supply and demand. No economy ever achieves exact economic equilibrium, but it is a good measure of the overall health of an economy.

## EQUITY

The true value of businesses, property, or assets after amounts owed in loans, mortgages, and liens are subtracted; also, the promise to share in profits and appreciation in the business, property, or assets. If you own a home valued at $500,000 and have a $300,000 mortgage, you have $200,000 of equity in the home. If the home's value increases by $50,000, the equity increases to $250,000. However, if the home's value decreases by $50,000, the equity drops to $150,000.

## EXPORT

To sell products and services to other countries. A country has a favorable balance of trade if exports are greater than imports, and unfavorable if the reverse is true. A positive balance is known as a trade surplus.

## EXPROPRIATION

By right of eminent domain, a government's taking legal ownership or possession of a building or land for public use. Outside the realm of eminent domain, to expropriate is to take possession and claim as one's own including anything from ideas, money, promotions, homes, lands, etc. From the Latin *expropriates,* meaning "to deprive of property."

## FEDERALISM

The sharing of governing power between a single national governing body (the federal government) and state or regional governments. Both the federal and state governments have their own executive, legislative, and judicial branches as well as the power to assess taxes. Jurisdiction between state and federal matters is determined by various state and federal laws.

## HOLDING COMPANY

A company that owns stocks in several different companies. It is not involved in the day-to-day operations of the companies that it holds, or owns. The holding company owns the majority of stock in the other companies and therefore controls them under its management.

## IMPERIALISM

A system in which a strong nation dominates weaker nations and exploits them for their wealth and natural resources. As the stronger nation maintains a presence in the weaker nation, its culture expands into the weaker nation as well.

## IMPORTS

Those goods of foreign manufacture that are sold within a country's borders. This can include movements of cash, capital, gold, investments, tourist spending, and other resources. Nations sometimes attempt to limit certain imports by imposing tariffs or erecting other trade barriers.

# INDIVIDUALISM

The idea that each person has worth and a contribution to make. In economics, the idea that citizens of a country should be as free as possible to exercise economic choice, resulting in a benefit to all citizens. The belief that as the individual seeks to enrich his or her life, he or she will lift others to higher levels of achievement by providing financial compensation through employment, as well as experience and training.

# INSIDER TRADING

Purchasing or selling stocks based on privileged information. It is illegal to acquire "inside" information that will impact the sales price of shares of stock and then purchase or sell those stocks.

# INVISIBLE HAND

The term coined by economist Adam Smith (1723–1790) in his 1776 book *The Wealth of Nations*. Smith said that people seeking their own economic self-interest benefit society more than if they tried to benefit society directly. Even when an individual selfishly pursues wealth and personal enrichment, many other people are benefited.

# ISOLATIONISM

A nation's policy to isolate itself from the affairs and conflicts of other nations. The idea that a nation is best served by focusing all its resources on strengthening itself. The downside to isolationism is that such a nation will not have access to global markets and, if attacked, will have no international political capital to call upon for help in its defense.

## JURISPRUDENCE

Philosophy of law and system of interpretation of the laws; system or body of laws of a country or group; interpretation and debate among the legal community of judges, lawyers, legal experts, and the courts on how their country's laws will impact society and the citizenry, and what new laws should be created and enforced.

## LAISSEZ-FAIRE

The idea that a government should be involved as little as possible in economic matters; the principle of government noninterference in commerce and allowing private interests to flourish. The term is French and means, roughly, allow "to act" or "let them do it."

## LAW OF DIMINISHING RETURNS

The tendency of production output to decrease as time goes on, all other things being equal. In economics, it is the rule that increasing one factor of production while holding others constant will result in lower per-unit returns over time. For example, adding more workers to a company may improve productivity. But as more and more workers are added, the company will become less efficient and per-unit profitability will fall.

## LIBERALISM

In politics today, the left-leaning movements of progressive parties or political parties pushing for reforms to benefit the middle class. Originally, liberalism referred to political movements promoting the rights and freedom of the individual, voting representation of the individual, and freedom from government oppression to pursue happiness.

## LIMITED LIABILITY CORPORATIONS

Companies legally register as limited liability corporations to avoid legal exposure in lawsuits. If a suit is filed against such a corporation, the plaintiff must sue the company as an organization and not the owners, stockholders, or other investors as individuals. When a business or corporation fails, limited liability holds that only the assets of the corporation and not the owners' assets can be liquidated to cover the business's debts.

## LIQUIDITY

Business assets that can be converted to cash; the ability to have enough cash to pay a company's operating expenses without having to sell fixed assets or equipment, buildings, etc.

## MACROECONOMICS

A subfield of economics that focuses on large economic issues. Macroeconomics deals with the overall economic performance of a country, including structure, market behavior, government spending, etc. Microeconomics deals with smaller specific areas of economic activity.

## MADISON AVENUE

Symbol for the advertising industry. For years, most of the national advertising agencies were located on Madison Avenue in New York City. From these agencies many memorable advertising campaigns were created. However, today, advertising agencies are located in many parts of New York City as well as in other large cities.

## MARKET ECONOMY

Another term for a capitalist economy; also called the free enterprise system or free market. The marketplace determines the price of products and services based on supply and demand. A market economy is the opposite of a command economy, in which the government owns and controls most of a country's industry and businesses.

## MARXISM

Political and economic theories of Karl Marx. Marx argued that throughout history the rich and powerful have exploited the masses of common workers. Over time the working class will struggle against the capitalists, resulting in the eventual overthrow of the capitalist system. The working class will institute a socialist form of government, leading eventually to a classless society.

## MICROECONOMICS

A field of economics that explains specific aspects of larger economic questions. Microeconomics deals with such areas of economic activity as rate of investment, commodities, exports, imports, etc. Microeconomics looks at individual markets as opposed to looking at all markets working together.

## MONETARISM

Monetarists attempt to control inflation by limiting the growth of a nation's money supply and not raising taxes. When a government prints more money, this inflates the currency because there is more money in the system. Under these conditions purchasing power declines. Monetarism attempts to find the ideal rate at which the monetary supply of a nation should grow.

## MONEY MARKET

The forum in which money is bought and sold. Term for all the markets in which money is loaned to governments, or businesses are bought and sold. Large institutions and governments can acquire cash from the money market for short-term expenses. Money markets are lower risk than investing in the higher-risk stock market, which can experience bearish as well as bullish trends.

# MULTILATERALISM

In political philosophy, when more than one nation or group of nations participates in an initiative that benefits all their countries. Multilateral means "many sided." Nations with divergent interests and views often work together toward a common solution such as increasing trade or negotiating treaties to protect natural resources.

# NATIONAL DEBT

Debt incurred by a country's central government when it borrows money to make up the deficit in its spending. State and regional governments can also incur debt. Governments borrow money from other countries by issuing government bonds or securities. Countries with less stability may borrow money from the World Bank or other global financial institutions. Government debt can be external, owed to foreign lenders, or internal, owed to lenders from its own country.

# NATIONALISM

Patriotism; devotion to the advancement of one's country; feelings of national pride. Sociologists have identified two possible causes for nationalists: a primordial perspective and a modernist perspective. The primordial view suggests that nationalism is an innate characteristic, which manifested in the earliest tribes that formed for survival through cooperation. The modernist view is that each nation is unique and develops based on the structures of a nation and its culture.

# NEOCOLONIALISM

When a strong country tries to assert its dominance over a weaker nation, but without direct colonization efforts; when a stronger nation exercises economic and political control over another country through extensive involvement in the economic interests of the weaker country. Neocolonialism replaced direct systems of colonization practiced by the British Empire in the eighteenth and nineteenth centuries.

# NEW YORK STOCK EXCHANGE (NYSE)

Also known as the big board, the NYSE on Wall Street in New York City was the largest stock exchange in the United States. On the stock exchange, investors can buy and sell stock in companies registered with the exchange. In the 1990s the NASDAQ, a stock exchange for technology companies, became the largest stock market in the United States.

# OPEC

Organization of Petroleum Exporting Countries (OPEC). An association of large oil-exporting interests and nations founded to set petroleum export pricing and policies. Members include African, Asian, and Middle Eastern countries of Algeria, Angola, Indonesia, Iran, Iraq, Kuwait, Libya, Nigeria, Qatar, Saudi Arabia, and the United Arab Emirates.

# PARKINSON'S LAW

Humorous statement that "work expands to fill the time allotted for its completion." Named for the author of the statement, British historian Cyril Northcote Parkinson (1909–1993), who in 1955 published one of his essays in the magazine *The Economist*. In his piece Parkinson mentions that as the British Empire drifted into decline, the number of employees at the Colonial Office increased. The statement has implications for a company's productivity, stressing the need for managers to manage effectively and motivate their work force.

# PARTNERSHIP

Under contract law, the terms and relationship of people as partners in a business, sharing joint ownership of that business. Under their operating agreement, the partners agree to share profits and losses of the venture. Some partnerships include investors who only contribute money to the venture and other partners who will provide the labor and/or management for the business.

## PER CAPITA

The average per citizen. For example, the country's per capita income was estimated at $35,000. Originated from Latin "by the head." Per capita is used to demonstrate statistically certain trends within a country.

## POPULISM

A political movement that purports to base its ideas on those of the people. Populism is often seen as an anti-intellectual political movement not supported by fact or reason. Demagoguery often characterizes populist movements. The term can also refer to a political strategy of appealing to the common people, such as when politicians attack wealthy citizens for not paying their fair share of taxes.

## PRODUCTIVITY

A measure of how much value is being produced by an enterprise; total output per one unit of total input. The higher the rate of productivity a company can deliver, the more products or services it can produce. Productivity also means generating more output while reducing costs; therefore, as companies increase productivity, they can become more profitable.

## PROFIT MOTIVE

Pursuit of profit to enrich oneself in business ventures; the motivation to bring new products and services to the marketplace. Pursuing profit entails investment and personal sacrifice of time and labor in hopes of the rewards.

## PROGRESSIVE TAX

The higher a person's income, the more taxes she is required to pay as a percentage of her income. People with lower incomes pay less in taxes as a percentage of their income than the wealthiest who pay the highest percentage of their income. A regressive tax has the opposite effect.

## PROTECTIVE TARIFF

A fine or custom duties levied against imported products that cause the importer to raise its prices. This is done to raise money for the government as well as to protect domestic businesses, which are not assessed the tariffs. In the United States, tariffs generated the largest source of income for the government from the founding of the country until World War I.

## REAL GROSS NATIONAL PRODUCT

A country's gross national product after it has been adjusted to reflect inflation. Gross national product (GNP) is the total value of all products and services a country produced in one year. GNP is similar to gross domestic product (GDP), though the GDP does not account for the money people make from foreign investments.

## REDISTRIBUTION

In politics and economics, the practice of reducing income inequalities through progressive taxation. Governments assess individuals in higher-income brackets more taxes as a percentage of income than lower-income individuals. Then through antipoverty programs and government assistance for food, utilities, housing, and education, the government redistributes this income.

## RIGHT-TO-WORK LAWS

In the United States, state laws that prohibit employers from refusing to hire someone who does not belong to a labor union. Advocates of such laws claim that in states where labor unions have a strong presence, right-to-work laws level the playing field for workers who do not belong to unions. Opponents argue that the purpose of these laws is to weaken and destroy unions.

## SOCIALISM

System in which the ownership and control of a country's means of production and resources is mostly under government control, omitting only a few private companies and individuals. The balance of ownership between government and private ownership can lean to heavy government ownership and light private ownership, or heavy private ownership with less government ownership. Many social theorists regard socialism as the stage between capitalism and Communism.

## STAGFLATION

A perfect storm of economic inflation and stagnation; when inflation has risen accompanied by high unemployment and slow growth in consumer spending. The catch-22 is that when people are unemployed they have less money to spend on goods and services, and less money to spend leads to more unemployment. The United States experienced stagflation in the late 1970s when the term "misery index" was coined. This was a combination of the inflation rate and unemployment rate.

## STOCKS

A company issues, or sells, shares to raise money for business expansion. Owning shares of stock allows the holders of the stock to receive dividends of company profits. By owning stock, a person owns a certain percentage of the company. Stockholders have the right to vote at stockholder meetings, which determine the direction the company will take.

## SUPPLY AND DEMAND

Supply and demand is the fundamental mechanism that sets prices in an economy. When the supply of a product or service is high and the demand for that product or service is low, the suppliers will drop their prices to entice individuals to purchase the product or service. The opposite is true when demand for a product or service is high and the supply for that product or service is low. With demand high, individuals are motivated to pay more to secure that product or service. There are, however, many other factors that influence pricing, including marketing and advertising, government regulation, etc.

## SUPPLY-SIDE ECONOMICS

The theory that government can stimulate the economy and encourage private investment by lowering taxes on businesses. Because companies exist to pursue profit, they will have more money to invest in new business ventures by paying less in taxes. As investment increases and more products and services are available, prices will drop and inflationary pressures will ease. Thus the focus is not on creating demand, but increasing supply. Supply-side economic policies were instituted by Ronald Reagan's presidential administration.

## TARIFFS

Customs or duties put in place by a government on imports and exports into or out of its borders. Tariffs are intended both as a source of revenue for the government and as a means of discouraging the import of certain goods to allow native businesses to thrive.

## TAX DEDUCTION

A business expense that is deducted from income in order to lower the amount of taxes paid. Tax deductions can be taken for charitable contributions, and for the cost of doing business. Once all tax deductions have been calculated, taxes are paid on the lower income amount.

## TECHNOCRACY

The theory from the 1920s that societal institutions should be restructured based on the ideas of scientists, engineers, and technology specialists. The state would be governed by experts in a variety of fields who would apply the best thinking and theories to shaping society. The idea gained momentum during the 1930s as a way to apply the latest scientific and economic theory to combat the Depression. Technocrats believed that businesses were not capable of reforming themselves to benefit the public will.

## TOTALITARIANISM

Control of a government by a dictatorial regime; "total" control of the state by the government. The term "totalitarian" was probably first used to refer to Benito Mussolini (1883–1945), the Italian Fascist leader. A totalitarian government takes control of economic and political activities and holds them in a firm grip. There is a similarity to a Communist government, but a totalitarian government is usually personality driven with the top leader visible in public.

## TREASURY BILLS

Bills issued by the U.S. government that mature after ninety days. T-bills, as they are also called, do not pay interest but are sold at a discount below their worth as indicated on the bill. The purpose of Treasury bills is to help the government raise money in the short-term. The U.S. Treasury Department auctions Treasury bills each week.

## UNILATERALISM

In politics, a single policy objective or action taken by only one nation. In law, a circumstance in which a contract is legally binding on only one party. Compare to multilateralism, when more than one nation or group of nations participates in an initiative that benefits all the countries. Multilateral means "many sided."

## WELFARE STATE

Nations in which people are partially or fully dependent on the government for the basic necessities of life. In the United States, programs such as Social Security, food stamps, and welfare assistance are part of the welfare state. States in which such programs exist are sometimes said to have mixed economies. Modern welfare states include Sweden, Norway, Denmark, Finland, and, to an extent, the United States. Today's welfare states aim to provide universal coverage for their citizens.

## WINDFALL PROFITS

A point in business when profits are larger than expected; company profitability higher than normal due to good luck in the market or from positive unforeseen circumstances; when something of value is blown to you as if by the wind.

## WORLD BANK

An institution created after World War II to fund infrastructure and economic development in underdeveloped countries. It has been criticized for attempting to impose Western-based economic systems on countries, which has sometimes led to dramatic failures. The bank has 185 members and is located in Washington, D.C.

# THINGS
## YOU SHOULD
## KNOW ABOUT
# ART &
# LITERATURE

66 The purpose of art is washing the dust of daily life off our souls. 99

— Pablo Picasso

66 All good books are alike in that they are truer than if they had really happened and after you are finished reading one you will feel that all that happened to you and afterwards it all belongs to you: the good and the bad, the ecstasy, the remorse, and sorrow, the people and the places and how the weather was. 99

— Ernest Hemingway

In this section you'll learn the 100 things you need to know about art and literature, from Greek mythology, to the great novels of all time, to trends in the art world. You will learn how abstract art is an artistic representation of objects but not as you and I perceive them. How *Moby Dick* explores themes of good and evil, and the existence of God. How *The Tragedy of Othello* by William Shakespeare includes themes of love, betrayal, and even racism. How Tolstoy considered *War and Peace* more a poem than a novel and many chapters a philosophical treatise rather than narrative storytelling. These ideas and many more are in this chapter.

## ABSALOM, ABSALOM

A 1936 novel by American writer William Faulkner (1897–1962). Absalom, a character from the Old Testament and King David's favorite son, rebelled against his father. In Faulkner's novel the main character is Thomas Sutpen, who, like Absalom, fights against the empire his father has built through slavery. The novel tells the story of three families in three different time periods: before the Civil War, during the war, and after its conclusion. Through these three periods, Faulkner describes the rise and fall of the plantation culture in the South.

## ABSTRACT ART

Artistic representation of objects but not as we perceive them. Abstract art manipulates the form of objects, breaking away from strict realism of form or outline. As new ideas entered the world stage in philosophy, religion, and science, abstract artists felt a freedom to express new ideas as well as break with traditional artistic styles.

## ACHILLES' HEEL

A major point of weakness; a weak spot. In Greek mythology, the hero Achilles, as an infant, is dipped in the river Styx by his mother, the nymph Thetis, to make him immortal. This makes him invulnerable except where she holds his heel. Achilles dies during the Trojan War when an arrow pierces his heel.

## ACROPOLIS

To protect from invaders, a citadel or city center built on a hill or cliff for defense. Many ancient Greek cities were built in this manner with the acropolis as the city center and the remainder of the city spreading out from there. The most famous acropolis is in Athens, Greece. Other similarly constructed cities include Edinburgh in Scotland and Jerusalem.

## THE ADVENTURES OF HUCKLEBERRY FINN

An 1884 novel by American writer Mark Twain (1835–1910). It is the first novel to be written in the vernacular language of the southern United States. The book is part satire and provides vivid descriptions of the people and culture along the Mississippi River. The novel's narrator, Huck Finn, tells of his adventures as a fugitive in company with a runaway slave, Jim. The novel provides a stark realism into the nature of racism in the south in the late nineteenth century.

## AESOP'S FABLES

Some of the world's first stories that provided a means of teaching moral principles. The fables' main characters are animals, as in "The Fox and the Grapes." Aesop is believed to have been a slave in ancient Greece who lived in the fifth century B.C.E. Modern scholars believe that Aesop probably did not invent all the fables attributed to him, but rather he borrowed from other sources.

## AN AMERICAN TRAGEDY

A 1925 novel by American writer Theodore Dreiser (1871–1945). Clyde Griffiths works his way from poverty to wealth through duplicitous schemes. Although a poor farm girl working under his supervision in the factory is pregnant with his child, Clyde wishes to marry a rich socialite. When the girl threatens to reveal that she is pregnant, Clyde launches a plan to murder her. Dreiser based the characters of this novel on a murder and trial from 1906. Twenty-year-old Grace Brown was found dead at a lake in upstate New York. The resort owner who found her body was tried for the murder, convicted, and executed in the electric chair.

# ANIMAL FARM

This novel, published by English writer George Orwell (1903–1950) in 1945, is an allegory of the events leading to the Communist takeover of Russia in 1917 and the rise of Stalinist rule. The term "Orwellian" has come to mean totalitarian government systems in which the government exercises its authority by use of language as well as force.

# ANNA KARENINA

An 1876 novel by Russian writer Lev (Leo) Tolstoy (1828–1910). The main character, Anna Karenina, becomes entangled in an affair with a handsome bachelor, Count Vronsky. The count offers to marry Anna, but she refuses based on the social customs of the aristocracy, and then in desperation throws herself under a train. The novel opens with the insightful statement by Tolstoy: "Happy families are all alike; every unhappy family is unhappy in its own way." American novelist William Faulkner considered *Anna Karenina* the greatest novel ever written.

# ANTIGONE

Antigone's name means "opposed to motherhood" or "against men." The offspring of the mythological King Oedipus's incestuous marriage, Antigone defies men's dominant role in Greek family structure. She defies her uncle, Creon, by arranging a burial for her traitorous brother Polynices when the law prohibits mourning for him. As punishment, she is buried alive. She is the heroine of a play of the same name written by Sophocles (ca. 497 B.C.E.–ca. 406 B.C.E.)

# APOLLO

Greek god of light, sun, and knowledge; also, god of medicine and healing, although he can also bring plagues and sickness. He is the leader of the muses and associated with music and poetry. Son of Zeus and Leto, he is the ideal of youth and athleticism to the Greeks. Apollo was a prophetic deity in ancient lore.

# APPLE OF DISCORD

A small matter that leads to a larger argument or debate. The term originated from Greek mythology when Eris, the goddess of discord, inscribes "To the fairest" on a golden apple and tosses it into the wedding party of Thetis and Peleus. Aphrodite, Athena, and Hera fight over the golden apple, and the argument among the three women leads to the Trojan War.

# ARABIAN NIGHTS

Also known as the *One Thousand and One Nights*, these tales are folklore from the Islamic Golden Age. The stories date back to ancient Arabic, Persian, and Mesopotamian sources. Popular stories include "The Seven Voyages of Sinbad the Sailor," "Aladdin's Lamp," and "Ali Baba and the Forty Thieves."

# ARGUS

In Greek mythology, the "all-seeing" giant, famed for his 100 eyes, serving as the guardian of the heifer-nymph Lo. Lo, a priestess of Hera and a nymph seduced by Zeus, turned into a heifer to escape detection. Hera sends Argus to guard Lo. Argus's numerous eyes allow him to sleep with only a few eyes closed, so he can be watchful in all situations.

# ATHENA

In Greek mythology, the goddess of wisdom, law, justice, and courage. Also known as the goddess of heroic adventures as she accompanies heroes on their conquests. In mythology, she represents the strategic part of war and often leads soldiers into battle. She is also the patroness of crafts such as weaving. The Athenians built the Parthenon in her honor.

## AUGEAN STABLES

Augeas is king of Elis. His stables house more than 1,000 immortal cattle and have not been cleaned in thirty years. Because the cattle are immortal, they produce vast amounts of manure. The task of cleaning the stables is thought impossible and given to Hercules by the gods as part of his punishment for slaying their sons. Thinking the task is impossible, Augeas promises the hero 10 percent of the cattle if he accomplishes the feat. Hercules cleverly diverts two rivers to do the job, but Augeas is furious at his success, and Hercules kills the king.

## BACCHUS

In Roman mythology, the god of the grape harvest and winemaking. Associated with the Greek god Dionysius, Bacchus is suggestive of pleasure and ecstasy. As a god he comes on the scene to free the people with wine, music, and dancing.

## BAROQUE

An artistic movement beginning in Rome around 1600 with a flowing, exaggerated architectural style intended to produce dramatic effect and grandeur. Baroque artists encouraged viewers' emotional involvement with religious symbols and themes in painting, sculpture, architecture, dance, and literature. Promoted by the Roman Catholic Church as a response to the Protestant Reformation, the popularity of this artistic style quickly spread through Europe.

## BASILICA

Originally a public building or gathering place in a Roman city located in the forum or town center. After the conversion of the empire to Christianity, many of these buildings became churches. In modern usage, the term generally refers to a church. Many Catholic basilicas around the world have become the object of pilgrimages such as St. Peter's Basilica in Vatican City or the Basilica of Maxentius in Rome.

# BAS-RELIEF

An artistic, three-dimensional image that projects off a flat surface to show depth—usually carvings, sculpture, or metal works to show form. First used in the early Renaissance, this technique is exemplified by the raised heads of presidents on American coinage.

# BAUHAUS

A German architectural design school, at its height from 1919 to 1933, which integrated fine arts with crafts. Walter Gropius's (1883–1969) concept was to create a total work of art in which all art forms could be expressed, including the architecture of the building. The movement was very influential on modern design and architecture but the school closed under Nazi pressure in 1933.

# *BEOWULF*

An Old English poem considered one of the earliest and most important works of Anglo-Saxon literature. The poem is thought to have been written between the years 800 and 1100; the author is anonymous. The hero Beowulf helps the king of the Danes defend the mead hall from the monster Grendel. After slaying Grendel, the hero confronts the monster's mother and defeats her. As the hero, Beowulf proves his strength against supernatural forces and impossible odds.

# *BLEAK HOUSE*

An 1852 novel by English writer Charles Dickens (1812–1870). The novel centers on a legal case, *Jarndyce v. Jarndyce*, in which there is one testator but several wills. The protracted lawsuit is so drawn out that eventually its costs consume the entire estate, leaving the heirs with nothing. Dickens drew on his experience as a law clerk, and the novel levels many criticisms at the British legal system. Critics consider *Bleak House* Dickens's best-crafted novel with many subplots and minor characters.

## BOHEMIANISM

Lifestyle outside society's conventional norms, usually as part of a small group of people pursuing music, painting, literature, and so on; also refers to wanderers or to someone not having permanent ties to family or location. The term was first used to refer to artists, writers, and actors in European cities living among the lower classes. Bohemians often show disdain for the wealthy and worldly pursuits.

## BRAVE NEW WORLD

When someone says we live in a "brave new world," they are referring to a society that is advancing new ideas in science and technology but at the expense of genuine human relations. Aldous Huxley (1894–1963) published his dystopic novel in England in 1932. Set in the year 2540, when sleep-learning and new ideas in human reproduction mold a new society, the novel presents a vision of a society in which humans have become detached from love. The Modern Library ranks *Brave New World* fifth on the list of 100 best novels of the twentieth century.

## THE BROTHERS KARAMAZOV

Novel published in 1880 by Russian writer Fyodor Dostoyevsky (1821–1881). The book tells the story of the murder trial of one of four brothers accused of killing their father. Themes of the novel include morality and ethics, freedom of choice, and a person's ability to believe and exercise faith in God. Dostoyevsky is known for his cutting psychological analysis of his characters. His work provides insights into their motivations as they are faced with moral and ethical considerations.

# CRIME AND PUNISHMENT

Russian novelist Fyodor Dostoyevsky's great novel. Rodion Raskolnikov, the novel's main character, hatches a plan to murder a dishonest pawnbroker and rob her. He justifies the crime by telling himself that he can use the money for good and eliminate a reprobate. Convincing himself that the murder is for a higher purpose, he reflects on the life of Napoleon Bonaparte. He also rationalizes his pursuit to test if people are capable of such acts. In the end, having committed the murder, he repents, turns himself in, and redeems himself in exile.

# CATCH-22

A situation wherein a person is caught between two contradictory sets of imperatives. The term comes from the novel by Joseph Heller (1923–1999) of the same name, set during World War II. U.S. Air Force Captain John Yossarian, the novel's main character, wants to go home, having completed the required number of missions. When he asks the base doctor to ground him because he's crazy, Doc tells him he can't ground him because anyone who wants to get out of combat by being grounded is obviously sane.

# CATCHER IN THE RYE

A novel about teenage disillusionment and rebellion by J. D. Salinger (1919–2010). Holden Caulfield, the novel's seventeen-year-old protagonist, rehearses from a hospital the events leading to his breakdown. The novel deals with themes of identity development, loneliness, and teenage angst.

# CASSANDRA

In Greek mythology, Apollo gives Cassandra the gift of prophecy for her charms and beauty. But when she denies Apollo in his temple, he commands that her predictions will not be believed. Because of this, she is known as a tragic figure whose divinations are nonsensical but later prove correct.

# CATHARSIS

A deep emotional release of pent-up feelings or tensions, sometimes through creating or experiencing art. In psychology, the release of pent-up emotions, which can provide insights and clarification into what is bothering you.

# CHIMERA

In Greek mythology, a fire-breathing monster (part serpent, part lion, and part goat), which ravages the countryside. The term now means something terrible that exists only in the imagination. Chimera also refers to a genetically engineered animal. In medieval art, chimerical figures represent evil or harmful forces in nature.

# CUBISM

A painting or sculptural style emphasizing formal structure of geometrical forms over those found in nature. This avant-garde artistic movement broke up objects so they could be viewed simultaneously from multiple perspectives. Developed by Pablo Picasso (1881–1973) and Georges Braque (1882–1963) in the early twentieth century, cubism remains one of the most influential developments in the artistic world.

# DANTE'S *INFERNO*

The first part of Dante's *Divine Comedy*, a poem that tells the tale of Dante Alighieri's (1265–1321) journey through Hell, Purgatory, and Heaven. Hell consists of nine circles in which the souls of the damned suffer, paying for their sins. Each circle represents a class of sins, including lust, gluttony, greed, anger, heresy, violence, fraud, and finally treachery. Through irony, Dante cleverly relates the form of punishment to each class of sins.

# DON QUIXOTE

Fully titled, *The Ingenious Gentleman Don Quixote of La Mancha,* Miguel de Cervantes' (1547–1616) novel traces the overly romantic pursuits of Alonso Quijano, the novel's main character. The impressionable Alonso sets out to re-enact the chivalrous acts of knights of old as found in the books he reads. Under the assumed name of Don Quixote, Alonso ventures out into the real world where his unsuppressed romantic nature confronts the decidedly unromantic reality of his surroundings. The novel was published in two volumes, in the years 1605 and 1615. The word "quixotic" has come to mean extremely chivalrous or romantic, though impractical.

# ELECTRA

In Aeschylus's (ca. 525 B.C.E.–ca. 426 B.C.E.) *The Oresteia,* Electra persuades her brother, Orestes, to avenge their father's murder by killing their mother and her lover. In psychology in the early twentieth century, an Electra complex refers to the tendency of daughters to feel unconscious attraction toward their fathers and dislike toward their mothers.

# ELYSIAN FIELDS

A state or place of perfect happiness; paradisiacal state of the dead. In Greek mythology, the fields are the final resting place of heroic and honorable souls.

# EXCALIBUR

Legendary sword of King Arthur. In some versions of the legend, by pulling the sword out of a stone, he proves his right to rule England. In other versions, he is given Excalibur by the Lady of the Lake. Throughout Arthur's life, the sword is associated with magical powers and Arthur's prowess as king and warrior.

# EXPRESSIONISM

Originating in the early twentieth century, a modern-art movement that presents art in a completely subjective perspective with exaggerated emotion in order to generate new ideas and feelings. Expressionism is found in literature, painting, theater, dance, and film. Among the best-known examples is *The Scream*, a painting by Edvard Munch (1863–1944). In literature, people's perceptions of events and objects are distorted for dramatic effect.

# FABIAN TACTICS

Use of evasion and delaying tactics, instead of direct confrontation, to wear down an opponent; named for ancient Roman general Fabius (ca. 280 B.C.E.–203 B.C.E.) who generally avoided a full frontal attack during the Second Punic War. Rather he harassed the enemy through night raids and skirmishes, disrupting supply chains, and otherwise making things difficult for them. Fabian tactics are commonly used in lawsuits as both sides delay and level false allegations to wear each other down.

# FALL OF MAN

Pertains to the Christian doctrine of man's fall from grace to his current mortal state. After Adam and Eve partook of the forbidden fruit, they were cast out of the paradisiacal Garden of Eden, marking humankind's entrance into a fallen world and bringing death into the world. Christians believe this first sin, or Original Sin, is transmitted to their descendants.

# FAUSTIAN BARGAIN

A deal with the devil; willingness to sacrifice that which is most precious for youth and beauty, limitless power, or knowledge. Faust gives Mephistopheles, the devil, his soul for hidden knowledge. This bargain is perilous since at some point the devil will exact his price. Some attribute a person's remarkable human accomplishments not to one's natural abilities, but—jokingly—to a Faustian bargain.

# FUNCTIONALISM

A twentieth-century design movement stressing that buildings and furniture should be designed based on their purpose. Functionalism also has applications in philosophy and sociology. In philosophy, functionalism is the idea that desires, thoughts, beliefs, and other mental states derive from their functions. In sociology, structural functionalism studies culture and society as a system of interdependent parts that work together to maintain stability.

# GOLDEN FLEECE

A Greek myth. A winged ram's fleece of pure gold is kept in a kingdom by the Black Sea. The hero Jason and his companions, the Argonauts, make a voyage to obtain it in order that Jason can justify his claim to the throne of Iolcus.

# GORDIAN KNOT

Midas, son of Gordias, the king of the Phrygians (a minor kingdom in ancient Asia) tied the Gordian Knot. The myth says that whoever unties the knot can rightfully rule Asia. Alexander the Great, rather than attempt to untie it, sliced through the knot with his sword. Thus the term "cutting the Gordian Knot" has come to mean acting confidently and quickly to solve an apparently intractable problem.

# GOTHIC

An architectural style of the twelfth through the sixteenth centuries, it originated in France and spread through Europe. It once predominated in cathedrals, featuring high arches, ribbed vaults, and flying buttresses. Notre Dame de Paris and Chartres are two cathedrals built in this style. In literature and film, gothic themes have been preoccupied with gloominess, terror, and the supernatural.

## THE GREAT GATSBY

A novel by F. Scott Fitzgerald set during the decade of the Roaring Twenties in America. It captures the essence of post–World War I prosperity and people's search for meaning in that time. Fitzgerald said, "The whole burden of Gatsby is the loss of those illusions that give such color to the world that you don't care whether things are true or false as long as they partake of the magical glory."

## HAMLET

Tragedy written by William Shakespeare (1564–1616) exploring themes of madness, revenge, incest, and morality. Prince Hamlet seeks revenge for the murder of his father, King Hamlet, by his uncle Claudius, who has married Prince Hamlet's mother, Gertrude, and taken the throne. One of Shakespeare's greatest works, *Hamlet* raises religious and philosophical questions concerning existentialism and relativism. It is one of the most quoted works in the English language.

## HERCULEAN

Possessing or requiring great strength. A herculean effort is a daunting task. The term derives from the myth of Hercules and his great strength and bravery for accomplishing twelve labors. These include slaying the Nemean lion, capturing the golden hind of Artemis, stealing the mares of Diomedes, and other challenging tasks.

## HOLY GRAIL

A medieval legend that Joseph of Arimathea brought the cup or bowl used by Jesus Christ at the Last Supper to Britain. (An alternate theory is that Joseph used the cup to catch Christ's blood as he was dying on the cross.) According to the Arthurian legends, many knights sought the Holy Grail for its supernatural power to bring a person into communion with the divine. Sir Galahad, at last, found the grail, the only one of the knights to do so.

## ICARUS

A character from Greek mythology. With wings made of feathers and wax, Icarus and his father, Daedalus, attempt to escape from Crete. Although Daedalus warns him not to fly too close to the sun, Icarus disobeys, the wax melts, and he plunges to his death in the Aegean Sea. Hence, Icarus is associated with the impetuousness and inexperience of youth.

## THE ILIAD

Homer's epic poem about an episode during the ten-year siege of Troy by the Greeks, although it covers only several weeks of the war's final year. The Greeks led by Agamemnon seek to avenge the Trojans for the abduction of Helen by Paris, the son of the Trojan king Priam. In the end, the Greeks successfully plunder and burn Troy. *The Iliad* is often paired with Homer's *The Odyssey* as two of the most influential works of literature.

## IMPRESSIONISM

An artistic movement of the nineteenth century. Impressionists painted with bright colors and short brushstrokes to represent the play of light on objects. The artists wanted to record experience as fleeting impressions bathed by natural light, emphasizing immediate aspects of objects without attention to too many details. Impressionist painters include Claude Monet (1840–1926), Pierre-Auguste Renoir (1841–1919), and Alfred Sisley (1839–1899).

## "INVICTUS"

Poem by English poet William Henley (1849–1903) about the virtues of stoicism. At seventeen, to save his life, Henley's leg was amputated below the knee because of tuberculosis of the bone. As he was recovering from the surgery he penned this poem, which is famous for its optimism in the face of severe challenges.

> *Out of the night that covers me,*
>
> *Black as the Pit from pole to pole,*
>
> *I thank whatever gods may be,*
>
> *For my unconquerable soul.*

It is a remarkably well written poem for someone so young.

## JANUS

Ancient Roman god of passageways and doorways, he is represented as having one head but with two bearded faces looking in opposite directions. Symbolic of new beginnings and of the setting of the sun closing one day and rising to open a new day.

## KITSCH

Art (or any other object) that looks expensive but is in poor taste and lacking substance. Kitsch objects are often designed for popular appeal and are usually gaudy. The term originates from the German *kitschen*, "to smear." The famous series of paintings depicting dogs playing poker by C. M. Coolidge (1844–1934) is an example of kitschy art.

## THE LAST OF THE MOHICANS

An 1826 novel by American writer James Fenimore Cooper (1789–1851). During the French and Indian War, Uncas, an Indian, helps a family of British settlers. This early American novel was one of the most popular English-language novels of its time. Cooper actually confused the Mohegan and Mahican Indian tribes, but this made no difference to the appeal of the novel. Nor was Uncas the last of the Mohicans. Both tribes exist today.

## LEITMOTIF

A musical theme that recurs frequently throughout a work of art, most commonly in opera and classical music. *Leitmotiv* is the German word for "leading motif." According to *Elson's Music Dictionary*, "The leitmotif must be characteristic of the person or thing it is intended to represent."

## MACBETH

The darkest tragedy written by William Shakespeare in which Macbeth, a Scottish noble, murders the king to obtain his throne. At the prodding of his wife and acting on the prophecy of three witches, Macbeth hatches an ambitious scheme to murder the monarch, while King Duncan is his guest. To further his power, while reigning as king, Macbeth continues to murder, sending the country into civil war. As a result of his moral descent, he loses everything, including, eventually, his life.

## METAMORPHOSES

A group of legends told in poetic form by the Roman poet Ovid (43 B.C.E.–ca. C.E. 17). The poems, which tell numerous stories from mythology, all contain a theme of change. The title is related to the word "metamorphosis," meaning "transformation."

## MOBY DICK

Herman Melville's (1819–1891) masterpiece written in the year 1851 in which the main character, Captain Ahab, in his madness pursues the giant white whale Moby Dick with great force and frenzy. On a previous whaling hunt, Moby Dick thrashed Captain Ahab's boat and bit off a portion of his leg. Revenge drives the captain in his quest. The novel explores various themes of good and evil, the existence of God, and the nature of obsession.

## MONA LISA

Said to be "the best known, the most visited, the most written about, the most sung about, the most parodied work of art in the world," according to author John Lichfield in his book *The Moving of the Mona Lisa*. Painted by Leonardo da Vinci (1452–1519) between 1503 and 1506, it is believed to be a portrait painting of Lisa Gherardini, wife of a Florentine cloth merchant. It was first acquired by the French king Francis I (1494–1547) and is today on display at the Louvre in France. Mona Lisa's slight and ambiguous smile has fascinated many people with its mixture of mystery and sorrow.

## MORPHEUS

In Greek mythology, the god of sleep and dreams. Since he appeared in dreams, Morpheus could take any human form. In the Greek language, the word means "the maker of shapes." The drug morphine derives its name from Morpheus. The land of dreams was believed to be located near the underworld near the dominion of Night.

## MUSES

In Greek mythology, sister goddesses who oversaw creative and artistic acts and passions. The muses—Aoide (song), Melete (meditation), and Mneme (memory)—were sent to inspire the Greek poets, actors, artists, and philosophers. Today, to call upon the muses means to search for the unfolding of your genius. To muse over a subject is to ponder deeply or meditate upon it.

## NARCISSUS

In Greek mythology, a young man who falls in love with his own reflection. Obsessed with himself, he pines away his days unable to tear himself away from his reflection in a pond, wasting away and finally transforming into a flower. Flowers with yellow or white petals in a cup-shape are from the genus *Narcissus*, similar to a daffodil. A narcissistic person is filled with vanity and extreme self-love to the point of rejecting all other people's needs and desires.

## *THE ODYSSEY*

Homer's epic poem of Odysseus's ten-year attempt to return home after the Trojan War. An odyssey is any long series of adventures with setbacks, trials, and hardship. Since Odysseus is assumed dead, his wife, Penelope, must deal with a group of suitors. Meanwhile, Odysseus's trials include near death on the island of the Cyclopes, the Laestrygonians (giants who eat people), the land of the dead, temptation by the sirens, imprisonment by the sorceress Circe, and other dangers as he makes his way home.

# OEDIPUS

A mythical king of Thebes who unknowingly murders his father and marries his mother. To pay penance, he blinds himself and goes into exile. An oracle predicts that King Laius of Thebes, Oedipus's father, would be killed by his own son. To prevent this, Laius orders that the infant Oedipus be taken to a mountaintop and left to die. However, the baby is rescued by a shepherd. As an adult, Oedipus meets and kills a man in a quarrel (the man being the king and, unknown to Oedipus, his father). Oedipus goes on to Thebes and saves the city from the Sphinx. He is made king and marries the dead king's widow, his mother.

# OTHELLO

A tragedy by William Shakespeare, which deals with themes of love, betrayal, and racism. The villainous Iago convinces Othello, a famous general, that Desdemona, Othello's wife, has been unfaithful. At the conclusion of the play, Othello suffocates Desdemona. Finally realizing her innocence, Othello attacks and kills Iago.

# PANDORA'S BOX

In Greek mythology, Pandora, the first woman, is given a box by Zeus with strict instructions not to open it. Curious, Pandora opens the box and the evils and suffering that afflict humankind escape into the world. However, also in the box is Hope. The myth is similar to the Adam and Eve story from Genesis. To open a Pandora's box is to act in a way that sets events in motion with disastrous consequences.

## PARADISE LOST

Epic poem by John Milton (1608–1674) about the fall of man as outlined in the Bible. A religious man, Milton's poem tells of Satan's rebellion in the war in heaven and his fall to the earth. It also tells the story of the creation of Adam and Eve and their subsequent fall and expulsion from the Garden of Eden. Milton stated that the purpose of the poem was to "justify the ways of God to man."

## PHOENIX

A mythical bird that lived 500 years and then burned itself on a funeral pyre, only to re-emerge from the ashes as a chick. The phoenix is a symbol of reborn hope and new beginnings; a person or thing that has been restored after suffering loses; rising from the ashes to rebirth.

## PLATO'S ACADEMY

Influential school founded by Plato in Greece around 387 B.C.E. in Athens. Rather than espousing a particular doctrine, Plato posed problems to his students for study and debate. Scholars assume that much of the discussions came from the ideas in Plato's writings in *The Republic*. Aristotle (384 B.C.E.–322 B.C.E.) studied under Plato for twenty years before starting his own school, the Lyceum.

## PRIMITIVISM

The belief that earlier or primitive cultures are superior to contemporary cultures or society. Primitives suggest that modern civilization should be scrapped in favor of the simpler agrarian lifestyle of the past. In art, the movement called primitivism arose in the late nineteenth century among such artists as Paul Gauguin (1848–1903) and Henri Rousseau (1844–1910).

## PROCRUSTES

In Greek mythology, a giant and a thief who place travelers on an iron bed. If they are shorter than the bed, he stretches their arms and legs; if they are longer, he amputates those appendages. Thus a procrustean approach is one that tries to force an idea into a predetermined pattern of belief.

## PRODIGAL SON

This parable from the New Testament tells of a younger son who hastily took his inheritance and spent it foolishly. Impoverished, he swallowed his pride and returned home to the open arms of his father. The term refers to someone who returns home after experiencing the bitterness of life's lessons.

## PROMETHEUS

A Titan who teaches humankind various arts and skills. Legend has it that he shapes humans out of clay and steals fire from the heavens to give to them. For stealing fire from Mount Olympus, he is chained to a rock where an eagle eternally picks at his liver. He is at last released by Hercules. Prometheus is a symbol of aloneness and resistance to authority as well as the human quest for knowledge.

## PROMISED LAND

The Bible's characterization of the land of Canaan, which it said was a land flowing with milk and honey, promised by God to the Israelites. The region of Canaan was promised first to the biblical patriarch Abraham. The Israelites finally possessed Canaan after wandering in the desert for forty years with Moses and then conquering the tribes of people who lived in Canaan. The phrase can refer to a place that one longs for and believes will provide happiness and respite.

## PSYCHE

In Roman mythology, a beautiful girl loved by Cupid who becomes the personification of the soul; the human soul, spirit, or mind or breath of life; the invisible directing principle of a person; the motivating force or mental structure of a person. Psyche is visited in the night by Cupid who tells her she must not try to see him. When she holds a lamp to see his face, oil spills on Cupid and he flees. After Psyche performs tasks set by Cupid's mother, she is made immortal and marries Cupid.

## PYGMALION

A goldsmith of Cyprus who carves a statue of a young girl and falls in love with it. In response to his prayers that he find a woman to love, Aphrodite brings the statue to life. In some versions of the story, Pygmalion is a misogynist who hates women, but he cherishes his newfound love.

## *THE RED BADGE OF COURAGE*

A Civil War novel by American writer Stephen Crane (1871–1900). The story's main character, Henry Fleming, a Union soldier, flees from a battle. Embarrassed and ashamed by his action, he desires a red badge of courage—that is, a wound. He later rejoins his regiment as a standard bearer. The novel is considered remarkable for its accurate detail and portrayal of Civil War battles, even though Crane did not witness the war. He was able to piece together such vivid accounts by talking to veterans of the war.

## REQUIEM

In the Roman Catholic Church, a mass conducted for the souls of the dead. Not necessarily a funeral for one person, but a service for the repose of the dead. Also a musical hymn or service performed at a funeral.

# ROCOCO

Architectural style from France from the early eighteenth century. It features elegant and refined details such as ornate shell decorations and foliage. Rococo styles evolved from the baroque style of art and architecture.

# ROMANESQUE

European architectural style popular from the ninth to twelfth centuries. Romanesque buildings were made with walls of heavy masonry pierced by round arches and narrow vaults. Used widely in church towers. Romanesque combined architectural features from the Roman and Byzantine empires, particularly the Roman arch.

# ROMANTICISM

Beginning in the mid-nineteenth century, a movement in literature and art that stressed emotion, free-flowing imagination, and freedom from rules and constraints. The Romantics, rebelling against the classicism of the eighteenth century, also viewed nature as wild and untamed. Romantic poets included such figures as Lord Byron (1788–1824) and Percy Shelley (1792–1822).

# *THE SCARLET LETTER*

A nineteenth-century American novel by Nathaniel Hawthorne (1804–1864). After her pregnancy becomes known in Puritan Boston where she lives, Hester Prynne is forced to wear a scarlet *A* to let the townspeople know that she is an adulteress. As she is unwilling to reveal the father of the child, the townspeople are left to gossip among themselves. At last the father is revealed—the local minister, Arthur Dimmesdale—when his guilt has produced a scarlet *A* on his flesh. Themes of the novel include sin, guilt, and hypocrisy.

## SIRENS

In Greek mythology, these creatures, part woman and part bird, would sing seductively from the cliffs, producing a trance-like effect on sailors passing by. If they allow themselves to listen, the sailors could not help but steer their ships toward the beautiful voices and the dangerous cliffs, eventually crashing on the rocks. Siren is used to describe a beautiful woman (or anything beautiful) who beguiles men and leads to their harm.

## SISTINE CHAPEL CEILING

Masterwork of Michelangelo (1475–1564), who at the behest of Pope Julius II (1443–1513) painted the ceiling of the Sistine Chapel inside the Vatican between 1508 and 1512. After erecting scaffolding and making elaborate drawings of his designs, which he then transferred to the ceiling, Michelangelo painted lying on his back for four years, 1508–1512. He painted nine scenes from the Bible's book of Genesis. The work is considered the high point of Renaissance art. The Sistine Chapel is the site of papal conclaves as well as other high-level meetings within the Catholic Church.

## *THE SOUND AND THE FURY*

A 1929 novel by American writer William Faulkner. The novel is about a once-wealthy southern family, the Compsons, and how they deal with losing their wealth and reputation in the new social order of the post–Civil War South. The novel is written in four sections, each of which tells the Compson family tale through the perspective of a different family member. The novel marks Faulkner's entry into stream-of-consciousness writing similar to that practiced by James Joyce (1882–1941). In one section of the novel, for instance, he relates the thoughts of a mentally retarded man with no direction to the timing of the events.

## SPIRITUALISM

The belief in a spirit essence that animates all life forms; the doctrine that after death, disembodied spirits can influence and communicate with those within the mortal sphere. In metaphysics, spiritualism is the belief that the ultimate reality is spiritual or mind; in philosophy, spiritualism is the belief that the nature of reality to some extent contains an immaterial or spiritual substance.

## THE SUN ALSO RISES

A novel by Ernest Hemingway written after he served in World War I and was living in Paris with other young artists. The novel is set against the background of the Lost Generation of Americans following their disillusionment by World War I. The novel's main character is injured in the war and, due to his injury, is not able to live fully. Other characters in the novel have also been impacted by the war in one way or another.

## SURREALISM

In the twentieth century, paintings or literature that tries to represent, through symbols and distortions on reality, the subconscious or nonrational aspects of the mind. Salvador Dali's (1904–1989) painting *The Persistence of Memory*, which shows melting clocks in a desertlike landscape, challenges the perception that time is rigid, suggesting that the perception of time is more free-flowing and determined by the viewer.

## SWORD OF DAMOCLES

An impending disaster. According to one version of a Greek myth, Damocles, a courtier, is invited by the king to a banquet and seated under a sword that hangs by a single hair. The king thus delivers the message that Damocles is skating on thin ice. It is from this myth that the expression "hanging by a thread" originates.

## THE TRIAL

A 1925 novel by Franz Kafka (1883–1924). Although the crime that is the subject of the trial is never revealed, the novel tells the tale of a man, Josef K., the chief officer of a bank, arrested by an unapproachable authority. The events in the novel are illogical and it is as if Josef is living a nightmarish dream. The novel is about "everyman's" struggle for meaning and order in the world and the fight against human weakness. Kafka, in this and other works, depicts an almost-paranoid awareness of the shifting balances of power in society.

## TROJAN WAR

In Greek mythology, a war waged by the Greeks against the city of Troy. The cause of the war is the kidnapping of Helen, wife of a Greek king, by Paris, son of King Priam of Troy. The war lasts ten years and ends in the treachery of the wooden horse and the burning of Troy.

## ULYSSES

A novel by Irish author James Joyce published in 1922. Ulysses is the Latin form of Odysseus, and the novel is a modern-day retelling of the Greek poet Homer's *The Odyssey*. Characters in the novel stand in for characters in *The Odyssey*: Molly Bloom as Penelope, and Stephen Dedalus as Telemachus. The novel follows the main character, Leopold Bloom, through Dublin, Ireland, on June 16, 1904. The novel was controversial for its complex writing style and was banned for a time from the United States due to its graphic portrayal of sex.

## UNCLE TOM'S CABIN

An 1852 novel by American writer Harriet Beecher Stowe (1811–1896). The novel tells the dark and realistic story of life as a slave in the United States. The novel's main character, a slave, is finally beaten to death by his overseers. The novel was published prior to the Civil War and helped build antislavery public support.

## VANISHING POINT

The point in a drawing or painting where two parallel lines join together in the distance or on the horizon. The vanishing point is a key element of linear perspective, an art technique developed during the Renaissance. The phrase can also indicate the point of disappearance or extinction.

## *WALDEN*

"The mass of men lead lives of quiet desperation." So wrote Henry David Thoreau in *Walden*, a book in which he recounts his two years living alone at Walden Pond in Massachusetts. In the book he discussed his daily life in nature and the individual's ability to live outside and independent of society.

## *WAR AND PEACE*

A novel by Russian writer Leo Tolstoy. It recounts the history of several aristocratic Russian families and the impact on their lives from the Napoleonic invasion of 1812. It is written in great descriptive detail, and Tolstoy commented that the novel is more a poem than a novel. It is widely considered one of the greatest novels ever written, largely for its epic scale and complexity, as well as for its writing.

# 5

# THINGS
## YOU SHOULD
## KNOW ABOUT
## PEOPLE &
## CULTURE

" Culture is the process by which a person becomes all that they were created capable of being. "

## —Thomas Carlyle

In this chapter you'll learn the 100 things you need to know about people and culture from sports to music to film to social reformers. You will learn how Muhammad Ali was arrested for draft evasion and lost his boxing title, but appealed to the U.S. Supreme Court and won. How Alfred Hitchcock, one of the greatest and most ingenious filmmakers of all time, pioneered camera angles and other techniques to build suspenseful moments in his films. How Rosa Parks became the first lady of civil rights. How William Shakespeare is regarded as the greatest writer of all time. How Frank Lloyd Wright designed more than 1,000 buildings and oversaw the construction of 500 of them, with the buildings designed to be in harmony with the spirit of the environment. All that and more is here.

## AARON, HENRY (1934–)

One of the greatest baseball players of all time as well as one of the first African-American major league baseball players. Aaron played twenty-three seasons from 1954 to 1976 and was ranked the fifth best player on *Sporting News*'s list of the 100 best major league baseball players of all time. He surpassed Babe Ruth's home run record in 1974 by hitting his 715th career homer.

## ADDAMS, JANE (1860–1935)

One of the first social workers in the United States in the early twentieth century. She was awarded the Nobel Peace Prize in 1931. Addams worked to raise awareness for women's rights, especially issues relating to mothers and the public health. She founded the Hull House in Chicago, which took in European immigrants when they first arrived in the country.

## ALI, MUHAMMAD (1942–)

One of the greatest boxers of all time, winning the world-heavyweight championship at age twenty-two. Ali created controversy when he declared himself a conscientious objector based on his beliefs in Sunni Islam and opposition to the Vietnam War. He was arrested for draft evasion and lost his boxing title. He then appealed to the U.S. Supreme Court and won. In all, he won three world-heavyweight championships. He was widely known for his trash talking of opponents before a match.

## ALLEN, WOODY (1935–)

American screenwriter and director. He starred in many of his own films, including *Take the Money and Run, Annie Hall*, and *Manhattan. Annie Hall* won him four Oscars in 1977. He began his career as a comedian and developed the persona of a worrisome, neurotic intellectual that he portrayed on screen. The television network Comedy Central listed Allen as number 4 in the 100 greatest standup comics of all time.

## ANDERSEN, HANS CHRISTIAN  (1805–1875)

Storyteller famous for his fairytales, which appeal to adults and children alike and have been translated into 125 languages. His fairy tales include "The Emperor's New Clothes," "The Princess and the Pea," "Thumbelina," and "The Little Mermaid," all of which teach important moral lessons. Many of his fairy tales have been made into movies.

## ANGELOU, MAYA  (1928–)

African-American author, poet, and speaker, famous for writing about her childhood and experiences as a young black adult, particularly *I Know Why the Caged Bird Sings*. She has written autobiographies, essays, and poems as well as contributed to movies, plays, and television. She holds more than thirty honorary degrees.

## ARMSTRONG, LOUIS  (1901–1971)

Jazz trumpeter from New Orleans, influential in the birth of American jazz in the 1920s. He was also well known as a singer, with an instantly recognizable raspy voice. In a racially divided America, Armstrong appealed to both black and white audiences.

## ARMSTRONG, NEIL  (1930–2012)

First man to walk on the moon. Armstrong was the mission commander on *Apollo 11* and reached the moon on July 20, 1969. The following day he and Buzz Aldrin (1930–) spent more than two hours exploring the moon's surface. Armstrong said the famous words just before he stepped on the moon's surface: "That's one small step for a man, one giant leap for mankind."

## ASTAIRE, FRED (1899–1987)

American actor, dancer, and singer who made thirty-one musicals over a seventy-six-year period. His best-known dancing partner was Ginger Rogers (1911–1995). The two starred in ten films together. The American Film Institute ranked him fifth on their list of the greatest male stars of all time.

## AUDUBON, JOHN JAMES (1785–1851)

French-American naturalist and painter, famous for his painting and depictions of birds native to America. In his lifetime, he discovered twenty-five new species of birds. In 1827 he published a book titled *The Birds of America*. The National Audubon Society is named after him.

## BACH, JOHANN SEBASTIAN (1685–1750)

German composer in the baroque period. He is most renowned for his Brandenburg Concertos and skills at playing the organ. Bach's father was a musician and taught him how to play the harpsichord and violin, but it was at the organ that he most excelled. He taught music in Germany, as well as lived in Italy and France. After a decline, Bach's music regained popularity in the first part of the nineteenth century, and he is considered a giant of classical music.

## BARNUM, PHINEAS T. (1810–1891)

American entertainer and con man, as well as the founder of the circus that became Ringling Bros. and Barnum & Bailey. He had a reputation for promoting hoaxes on the American public and exploiting people in his circus, such as Tom Thumb, a little person. After financial collapse due to lawsuits and bad investments, Barnum became a public speaker on temperance in order to get back on stable financial ground.

## BEETHOVEN, LUDWIG VAN (1770–1827)

German composer and pianist and one of the most influential composers of all time. He wrote symphonies, sonatas, and concertos. At an early age he showed musical promise and was taught music by his father. Remarkably, although he lost his hearing in the last ten years of his life, he continued composing music, although he had to give up conducting and performing.

## BELL, ALEXANDER GRAHAM (1847–1922)

A scientist and innovator; inventor of the first workable telephone. Bell was awarded the first patent for the telephone in 1876. A scientist first, Bell also worked on discoveries in aeronautics and hydrofoils. Bell's mother and wife were deaf, which added to his determination as an inventor of the telephone and similar devices.

## BERLIN, IRVING (1888–1989)

Considered one of the most influential composers and songwriters of all time. He was born in Russia, but immigrated to America as a youth. He said he wrote music to "reach the heart of the average American." George Gershwin (1898–1937), another great composer, said that Berlin was the greatest songwriter who ever lived. He wrote more than 1,500 songs for movies, Broadway plays, and general listening and was nominated eight times for Academy Awards.

## BERNSTEIN, LEONARD (1918–1990)

American composer and conductor; director of the New York Philharmonic. As a composer he wrote the music for the Broadway musical *West Side Story*. He was one of the first American-born composers and conductors to match the stature of the foreign-born composers who immigrated to America. He became widely known to American audiences from his many television appearances.

# BONNIE AND CLYDE

Well-known bank robbers and outlaws in the United States in the late 1920s and early 1930s. Along with their gang, the duo held up small banks and stores in rural towns in the central United States. Bonnie Parker (1910–1934) and Clyde Barrow (1909–1934) were ambushed by law enforcement and killed on May 23, 1934. The newspapers at the time portrayed Bonnie Parker as a cigar-smoking, gun-wielding accomplice, though she actually played a much smaller role in the gang.

# BOTTICELLI, SANDRO (1445–1510)

Italian painter from the early Renaissance. He is best known for his works *Primavera* and *The Birth of Venus*. Botticelli was rediscovered by art critics in the late nineteenth century and is regarded as one of the master painters of the Florentine Renaissance. He painted under the patronage of Lorenzo de Medici, who represented the golden age of the early Renaissance.

# BRAHMS, JOHANNES (1833–1897)

German pianist and composer who resided in Vienna where he was prominent in the musical scene. An excellent pianist, he is one of the three big *B*s of classical music: Brahms, Beethoven, and Bach.

# BYRD, RICHARD (1888–1957)

American explorer who led the first expedition to reach the North and South poles by airplane. He flew over a portion of the Arctic Ocean and the Antarctic Plateau. He also received the Medal of Honor for his military service.

## CARTER, JAMES EARL (Jimmy) (1924–)

Thirty-ninth president of the United States (1977–1981). He created the Departments of Energy and Education. His presidency was marked by the Iran hostage crisis, an economic downturn, and an energy crisis, which prompted him to establish a national energy policy. Before entering public life he was a peanut farmer and U.S. naval officer. Following his presidency, he became an unofficial ambassador and a noted promoter of Habitat for Humanity. He was awarded the Nobel Peace Prize in 2002.

## CARVER, GEORGE WASHINGTON (1864–1943)

African-American inventor and educator. He may have been born a slave in Missouri. He was an agriculturalist who worked to modify peanut, cotton, and soybean crops, helping poor farmers plant these alternative crops as a source of income. He is best known for the 100 products made from peanuts that he developed and promoted including paints, plastics, dyes, gasoline, and more.

## CÉZANNE, PAUL (1839–1906)

French postimpressionist painter. He is credited with helping to bridge the gap between the nineteenth-century postimpressionist style and the new styles of twentieth-century painters such as Picasso. Cézanne's bold brushstrokes, his use of colors, and the geometric forms he employed in his compositions mark him out as a member of the postimpressionists.

## CHOPIN, FRÉDÉRIC (1810–1849)

Virtuoso pianist and romantic composer. Born in Poland, he was quickly recognized as a child prodigy. He settled in Paris, living there for nineteen years before his premature death at age thirty-nine. He gave only thirty performances in France, teaching piano and composing music mostly for piano.

# CLEVELAND, GROVER (1837–1908)

The only U.S. president to serve two nonconsecutive terms, he was both the twenty-second (1885–1889) and twenty-fourth (1893–1897) president. He was the only Democratic president from 1861 to 1913, during which time the Republican Party dominated politics. Economic disaster struck the country in his second term, giving the Republicans a landslide victory in the election of 1897.

# COOLIDGE, CALVIN (1872–1933)

Thirtieth president of the United States. He served as the governor of Massachusetts where he broke the Boston police strike in 1919. Known as a decisive leader, he became the vice-presidential nominee to President Warren Harding. When Harding died in office, Coolidge became president and was elected to a full term in 1924. Coolidge was a conservative politician who restored confidence in the presidency.

# COPLAND, AARON (1900–1990)

American composer and conductor. His greatest popularity was in the 1930s and 1940s, when he wrote such works as *Appalachian Spring* and *Fanfare for the Common Man*. Sometimes called the dean of American composers, Copland's music was considered to have a distinctive American sound, reminiscent of the West and the pioneering, inventive spirit of the country.

# DALÍ, SALVADOR (1804–1989)

Surrealist painter. Dalí was a leader of the surrealist movement, friends with such luminaries as Luis Buñuel (1900–1983) and André Breton (1896–1966). However, his support of General Francisco Franco (1872–1975) in the Spanish Civil War in the 1930s alienated him from many of his fellow artists. He was known for his beautiful draftsmanship as well as his outrageous behavior.

## DARROW, CLARENCE (1857–1938)

American civil rights lawyer. He defended John Scopes (1900–1970), a Tennessee schoolteacher, in the highly publicized 1925 Scopes monkey trial. Scopes had taught the theory of evolution in his high school science class, defying a state law prohibiting its teaching. Darrow switched from practicing corporate law to labor law during his career and was a founder of the American Civil Liberties Union.

## DEWEY, JOHN (1859–1952)

American educator, psychologist, and philosopher. He was a pragmatic philosopher; pragmatism espouses the idea of practicality as a mean for discovering truth and meaning. He was also an early twentieth-century progressive who believed that society needed to be reformed to provide more advantages to the underprivileged. He proposed many educational reforms for public schools.

## DILLINGER, JOHN (1903–1934)

American bank robber. During the Great Depression, Dillinger and his gang robbed banks and police stations. He was the most notorious criminal of his day, and the press sensationalized his crimes to sell newspapers. J. Edgar Hoover (1895–1972) used Dillinger's brazen crime sprees to secure the funds from Congress to develop a better-equipped Federal Bureau of Investigation (FBI). Dillinger was killed outside the Biograph Theater in Chicago as he drew a gun on FBI agents who were about to apprehend him.

## DU BOIS, WILLIAM EDWARD BURGHARDT (W. E. B.) (1868–1963)

Sociologist and civil rights activist. He was the first African American to earn a doctorate from Harvard and became a cofounder of the NAACP, the National Association for the Advancement of Colored People. He spent his career writing about civil rights issues, producing such important books as *The Souls of Black Folk* and *Black Reconstruction in America*.

## DYLAN, BOB (1941–)

Iconic singer and songwriter, who set the tone for the folk music revival of the 1960s. In that decade many of his songs captured the spirit of the flower-power generation with song titles such as "The Times They Are a-Changin'" and "Blowin' in the Wind." He was active in both the anti–Vietnam War movement and the civil rights movement.

## EDISON, THOMAS (1847–1931)

American inventor who created the first practical, long-lasting light bulb and many other inventions. He is also credited with inventing the first motion picture camera and record player. Edison held more than 1,000 patents.

## EISENHOWER, DWIGHT D. (1890–1969)

Thirty-fourth U.S. president (1953–1961). Eisenhower was easily elected based on his popularity as the five-star general who led the 1944 invasion of Normandy during World War II. He also served as military governor of the U.S. Occupation Zone after the war in Europe and served as chief of staff of the army under President Harry S. Truman. As president, he championed the interstate highway system as well as NASA.

## EMERSON, RALPH WALDO (1803–1882)

American philosopher, essayist, and lecturer. He was a transcendentalist philosopher who believed that reality can be discovered through intuitive thought processes, in flashes of spiritual insight. In his lectures, he spoke about the strength and importance of individualism. He was a leading figure in the Unitarian Church and the patron of such other transcendentalists as Henry David Thoreau (1817–1862) and Margaret Fuller (1810–1850).

## FERRARO, GERALDINE (1935–2011)

Democratic congresswoman who was the first woman to run for vice president of the United States. She was elected to the U.S. House of Representatives, representing New York City, in 1978. In Congress she worked on legislation for equal wages for women. Walter Mondale selected Ferraro as his running mate in his 1980 bid for the presidency against Ronald Reagan. Though the ticket lost, Ferraro remained vocal on many political issues.

## FITZGERALD, ELLA (1917–1996)

Known as the Queen of Jazz. She was famous for her vocal range of three octaves as well as for her exquisite tone. She won thirteen Grammy Awards and had a fifty-nine-year music career. In 1987 she received the National Medal of Arts from President Ronald Reagan.

## FORD, GERALD (1913–2006)

Thirty-eighth president of the United States (1974–1977). Served as Richard Nixon's (1913–1994) vice president after the resignation of Spiro Agnew (1918–1996) and became the president when Nixon resigned. Prior to his time in the White House, Ford served in Congress for twenty-five years, representing Michigan's fifth district. As president, Ford presided over the worst economy since the Great Depression. He also issued a presidential pardon to Richard Nixon for his involvement in Watergate, the scandal that brought down the Nixon presidency.

## FORD, HENRY (1863–1947)

American car manufacturer and founder of the Ford Motor Company. He is famous for his assembly line, which mass-produced cars efficiently, each worker on the line doing a particular job continuously throughout a shift. The assembly line greatly increased productivity in American industry and lowered production costs. Ford was successful because he manufactured a car the average American could afford, moving away from luxury cars and opening a large, untapped market. He became one of the richest men in the world and gave much of his fortune to his Ford Foundation.

## FRANK, ANNE (1929–1945)

Jewish girl who lived in the Netherlands during the German occupation. Her diary, found and published after her death, details her days in hiding from the Nazis in hidden rooms of her father's office building. The diary has been the subject of plays and movies, and is widely read in school to teach about the Holocaust. In 1945, her family was betrayed and taken to concentration camps where Anne died of typhus.

## GAUGUIN, PAUL (1848–1903)

French postimpressionist artist known for his use of color and his use of symbolism. He was an avant-garde painter, sculptor, and writer, whose work influenced Henri Matisse (1869–1954) and Picasso (1881–1973). Appreciation for Gauguin's work grew immensely in the years after his death.

## GERSHWIN, GEORGE (1898–1937)

American composer and pianist. The son of Russian immigrants, he composed many Broadway musicals including *Porgy and Bess, Strike Up the Band,* and *Of Thee I Sing,* as well as soundtracks for movies. Works such as *Rhapsody in Blue* showed the influence of jazz on his work. *Porgy and Bess* is now considered one of the most important operas of the twentieth century.

## GOLDWATER, BARRY (1909–1998)

U.S. presidential candidate in 1964, known as "Mr. Conservative." He was a five-term senator from Arizona between 1953 and 1987. His run for president is credited with helping to revive the conservative movement, although he lost to Lyndon Johnson (1908–1973). He fought against Johnson's Great Society programs, as he had fought early in his Senate career against the programs created by President Franklin Delano Roosevelt's New Deal.

# GRAHAM, BILLY (1918–)

America's most prominent Christian evangelist since 1949 when his sermons started to be broadcast on radio and television. He has been consulted by all presidents since Dwight D. Eisenhower. He was active in civil rights, and preached with Martin Luther King Jr. He bailed Dr. King out of jail several times. In his later years, he has been a supporter of conservative causes.

# GRANT, ULYSSES S. (1822–1885)

Eighteenth president of the United States (1869–1877). He was elected after serving as the general who helped the North defeat the South in the Civil War. As president, he led his fellow Republican politicians as they legislated what was left of the Confederacy and slavery out of existence. He supported the guarantee of voting rights for African Americans. Sadly, the latter part of his administration was marked by political scandal.

# HANDEL, GEORGE FRIDERIC (1685–1759)

German composer from the baroque period who wrote operas and concertos. Although born in Germany, he studied music and opera in Italy and then became a citizen of England, where he created three opera companies. His most performed work is the *Messiah*, which has become a Christmas standard.

# HEARST, WILLIAM RANDOLPH (1863–1951)

American newspaper publisher. He aggressively acquired newspapers and magazines across the United States, and in his quest for higher and higher circulation numbers, he encouraged his journalists to write sensational stories. Hearst eventually became the owner of the largest newspaper and magazine publishing company in the world. Orson Welles's (1915–1985) film *Citizen Kane* is based on Hearst's life.

# HISS, ALGER (1904–1996)

U.S. government official accused in 1948 of being a spy for the Soviet Union. He was convicted of perjury and spent more than three years in prison. A former Communist, Whittaker Chambers (1901–1961), testified before Congress and said on national radio that Hiss was a Communist while working as a government official. Hiss sued Chambers for defamation of character; however, Chambers produced evidence that he and Hiss had worked together, which lead to Hiss's perjury conviction. He continued to deny any involvement with the Communists for the rest of his life.

# HITCHCOCK, ALFRED (1899–1980)

One of the greatest and most ingenious filmmakers of all time. His films are psychological thrillers, notable for their twists and dark humor. After making films in his native England he came to Hollywood in 1939. He pioneered camera angles and other techniques to build suspenseful moments in his films, which dealt with crimes and murders. Notable movies include *Psycho, Strangers on a Train*, and *The Birds*. Hitchcock almost always made cameo appearances in his films.

# HOLMES, OLIVER WENDELL, JR. (1841–1935)

Supreme Court justice who served on the highest court in the United States from 1902 to 1932. According to the *Journal of Legal Studies*, he is cited more often than any other Supreme Court justice. Famous for his "clear and present danger" concept and its limits on freedom of speech, he was also known for exercising judicial restraint, meaning that judges should limit their own power and only strike down laws that are clearly unconstitutional.

# HOOVER, J. EDGAR (1895–1972)

Long-serving head of the FBI from 1924 to 1972. He introduced new crime-fighting and evidence-gathering techniques such as forensic labs and a centralized fingerprint database. However, Hoover was accused of going beyond the legal limits to obtain evidence. He created private files on politicians, as well as on millions of other citizens, and used these to blackmail government officials. President Harry Truman accused him of "turning the FBI into Hoover's secret police force."

# HUGO, VICTOR (1802–1885)

French novelist and poet who wrote such classics as *Les Misérables* and *Notre Dame de Paris (The Hunchback of Notre Dame)*. As a young man he was enamored of French high society and culture. But during his lifetime his opinions shifted as he experienced much of the social changes and political unrest at the heart of nineteenth-century French political life and culture. He is buried in the Pantheon, a mausoleum containing famous French men and women.

# JOHNSON, LYNDON BAINES (LBJ) (1908–1973)

Thirty-sixth president of the United States (1963–1969). After serving as the vice president in the Kennedy administration, he became the president after John F. Kennedy (1917–1963) was assassinated. He won a second presidential term in 1964. He was a Democrat from Texas and one of only a few people to serve as president, vice president, senator, and representative. Johnson is known as the designer of the Great Society, which significantly expanded federal benefits to low-income citizens.

## KEATS, JOHN (1795–1821)

One of the most well known English poets, he was a contemporary of other English romantics such as Lord Byron and Percy Shelley. Like many great artists, Keats was not appreciated until after his death. Today, he is known the world over for such poems as "On First Looking into Chapman's Homer," and "Ode on a Grecian Urn" and is read and studied widely.

## KENNEDY, JOHN F. (JFK) (1917–1963)

Thirty-fifth president of the United States (1961–1963). After serving as a lieutenant in the U.S. Navy, Kennedy was elected congressman representing Massachusetts's eleventh congressional district and then as a senator from that state. Elected president at forty-three, Kennedy was one of the youngest men ever to assume the office. Kennedy was assassinated on November 22, 1963, while on a visit to Dallas, Texas, an event still controversial after fifty years.

## KENNEDY, ROBERT (RFK) (1925–1968)

Democratic senator from New York and member of the politically powerful Kennedy family, he was the younger brother of President John Kennedy and served as U.S. attorney general during his brother's administration. A strong supporter of civil rights in the 1960s, he was assassinated while running for the Democratic Party's presidential nomination in 1968.

## KING, MARTIN LUTHER, JR. (1929–1968)

Civil rights leader and Baptist minister who used nonviolent resistance tactics of marches and sit-ins to battle discrimination. At a massive 1963 civil rights rally in Washington, his "I have a dream" speech spoke of a vision of equality for all races wherein a person should be judged by the content of his or her character, not by skin color. He was assassinated in Memphis, Tennessee, on April 4, 1968.

## KISSINGER, HENRY (1923–)

U.S. diplomat who served as secretary of state for Presidents Nixon and Ford. He believed in realpolitik, relying on the strength of the United States to push the country's agenda with other nations. He was strongly opposed to basing foreign policy on idealistic objectives. In dealing with the Communist governments of the Soviet Union and China, he followed a path of détente, resulting in President Nixon's 1972 visit to China. Kissinger received the Nobel Peace Prize in 1973, along with Le Duc Tho (1911–1990) of the People's Republic of Vietnam, who declined the prize.

## LEONARDO DA VINCI (1452–1519)

Artist, inventor, architect, scientist, astronomer, mathematician, and musician—the embodiment of the Renaissance. A true Renaissance man and believed by some to be the most talented person to have ever lived, he painted such masterworks as the *Mona Lisa* and *The Last Supper*. He is credited with designing the first helicopter and calculator, though neither invention would be built until centuries later. Many of his scientific theories, such as plate tectonics, hold true today.

## LINCOLN, ABRAHAM (1809–1865)

Sixteenth president of the United States (1861–1865), he signed the Emancipation Proclamation in 1863 that freed the slaves. He led the United States through the Civil War and eventually reunited the Northern and Southern states. Among his most memorable speeches was the Gettysburg Address, given to dedicate the national cemetery at the Civil War battlefield in Gettysburg, Pennsylvania. "Four score and seven years ago," he began, "our fathers brought forth on this continent a new nation, conceived in liberty and dedicated to the proposition that all men are created equal." He was assassinated in 1865.

# LONG, HUEY (1893–1935)

Southern populist politician and fortieth governor of the state of Louisiana. He served as governor from 1928 to 1932 and then as member of the U.S. Senate from 1932 to 1935 when he was assassinated. He was a progressive, though often dictatorial, politician who created his "Share Our Wealth" program with the slogan "Every Man a King." He supported raising taxes on the rich and then using that money to build public projects. He was widely regarded as a corrupt politician who did what it took to get things done.

# LUTHER, MARTIN (1483–1546)

German religious reformer. After raising substantial disagreements concerning doctrines of the Catholic Church, Luther was excommunicated and condemned as an outlaw. He argued that people are saved by faith alone and not good works. He also translated the Bible from Latin into German to enable people of his country to read it more easily. The religious movement that he initiated became known as Protestantism.

# MACARTHUR, DOUGLAS (1880–1964)

U.S. military commander. In World War I he became a brigadier general, and in World War II MacArthur served as the commander of the U.S. Army Forces in the Far East and then supreme commander of the southwest Pacific area. He accepted Japan's surrender and presided over the U.S. occupation of Japan. During the Korean War, he exceeded his orders and was recalled by President Truman.

# MALCOLM X (1925–1965)

Civil rights leader and minister in the Nation of Islam. Born Malcolm Little, he was a harsh voice in the civil rights movement, often leveling charges of racism against whites. Opponents accused him of preaching black supremacy and violence. While Martin Luther King Jr. called for integration, Malcolm X preached that whites would never accept black equality. He was assassinated in 1965.

## MANN, THOMAS (1875–1955)

German essayist and novelist. Mann's writing was deeply philosophical and psychological, and full of German and religious symbolism. When Hitler came to power in the early 1930s, Mann fled to Switzerland and then immigrated to the United States. He was the 1929 Nobel Prize laureate in literature. Among his best-known works are *Buddenbrooks, The Magic Mountain*, and *Doktor Faustus*.

## MCCARTHY, JOSEPH R. (1908–1957)

U.S. senator from Wisconsin famous for his campaigns in the 1950s to identify Communists working in the U.S. government. During the Cold War between the United States and the Soviet Union, McCarthy held a series of highly sensational congressional hearings claiming that the U.S. State Department and much of the administration were filled with spies. He was much maligned for his tactics and censored by the Senate in 1954. Today the term "McCarthyism" applies to any kind of witch hunt based on irresponsible accusations.

## MEAD, MARGARET (1901–1978)

American anthropologist. She lived among the people in Southeast Asia and the South Pacific, and studied those cultures' attitudes toward sex. Based on what she learned, she advocated for more sexual latitude within Western culture. Her writings had a profound impact on the sexual revolution of the 1960s, as well as on how people viewed other cultures. She made many appearances on television in the 1960s and 1970s.

## MENCKEN, H. L. (1880–1956)

Named one of the most influential authors, essayists, and satirists of the first half of the twentieth century. He wrote about American social life, politics, art, and literature in a witty tone. He was critical of Christianity and creationism, and anything related to anti-intellectual movements. He published his book series *The American Language*, which explained how English was spoken in different regions of the country. He did not support representative government, claiming that it allowed inferior men to dominate superior men.

## MENDELSSOHN, FELIX (1809–1847)

German composer and pianist in the romantic period. He was a musical prodigy, but his parents did not make any effort to promote his talents. He traveled through Europe and was especially popular in Great Britain. He composed symphonies, chamber music, and piano solos and wrote the music for *A Midsummer Night's Dream*.

## MONET, CLAUDE (1840–1926)

French impressionist painter. Considered one of the founders of the impressionist movement, he is widely famed for his numerous studies of water lilies. The name "impressionism" comes from one of Monet's paintings titled *Impression, Sunrise*. Impressionists attempted to capture the fleeting impressions of reality that we have.

## MOZART, WOLFGANG AMADEUS (1756–1791)

German composer and musical prodigy from the late eighteenth century. Mozart was a prolific composer, sometimes composing music mentally without instruments. His first composition was at age five. Early in his career he became well known but made little money. Many of his works that are popular today, such as *The Magic Flute*, were written near the end of his life. Over his lifetime, he produced more than 600 musical works.

## NIXON, RICHARD (1913–1994)

Thirty-seventh president of the United States (1969–1974). He was the only president to resign from office. He served in the U.S. Navy during World War II and as a congressional representative and senator representing California. From 1953 to 1961 he was Eisenhower's vice president. Nixon ended the United States' involvement in the Vietnam War in 1973 and opened new relations with China while negotiating a détente with the Soviet Union; this was a course correction from other U.S. presidents. Although re-elected in a landslide in 1972, his cover-up of the break-in at the Democratic Party national headquarters at the Watergate Hotel was the beginning of his downfall.

## OLIVIER, LAURENCE (1907–1989)

One of the most respected English actors and directors of the twentieth century. He played more than 120 acting roles in a career that spanned more than six decades. His work ranged from Shakespeare to dramatic films. He received two Oscars, Best Actor and Best Picture, for *Hamlet* in 1948. He is regarded as one of the most distinguished Shakespeare interpreters in the history of the theater. Spencer Tracy (1900–1967) said that he was "the greatest actor in the English-speaking world."

## PARKS, ROSA (1913–2005)

Civil rights icon who refused to give up her seat on a bus in 1955 in Montgomery, Alabama, after the bus driver requested that she move to the back of the bus and into the black section. This action sparked a citywide bus boycott, regarded as the beginning of the modern civil rights movement. Because of it, Parks has been referred to as the first lady of civil rights. At the time of the boycott, critics claimed that the incident had been a staged event, as Parks had received activist training and worked for the NAACP.

## PATTON, GEORGE (1885–1945)

U.S. Army general who served in World War II, leading troops in the European theater. Born into a military family, he attended the U.S. Military Academy. As a soldier his first experience in combat was in Mexico, chasing Pancho Villa (1878–1923). Patton served in World War I in the tank divisions and was wounded in the war. At the beginning of World War II, he commanded the U.S. Second Armored Division. Eventually, he led troops into Casablanca, Sicily, and Normandy and commanded the U.S. Third Army as it advanced across France toward Germany. He died in a car accident in 1945.

## PICASSO, PABLO (1881–1973)

Spanish painter and sculptor. Along with Georges Braque, he was a founder of the cubist school of art and is considered one of the greatest artists of the twentieth century. Although he was Spanish, he lived in France for most of his life. He was an exploratory artist, constantly experimenting with new styles. As a teenager Picasso painted realistic pictures, but in his twenties he began to experiment with form and techniques such as collage and constructed sculpture.

## POE, EDGAR ALLAN (1809–1849)

American author and poet who wrote about the dark and disturbing side of life. One of the first authors to write short stories, he was also a leading literary critic. His stories such as *The Narrative of Arthur Gordon Pym of Nantucket* were influential on early science fiction writers. He had a sad childhood: His father abandoned him and his mother, and then his mother died. A family from Richmond, Virginia, raised him but never adopted him. Poe began writing poetry after flunking out of West Point and slowly launched a literary career that saw only limited success. His most famous poem, "The Raven," brought him some recognition.

## REAGAN, RONALD (1911–2004)

The fortieth president of the United States (1981–1989). Prior to serving as president, Reagan worked in radio and then as an actor in Hollywood. Originally a Democrat, he became a conservative Republican in the 1950s. After serving as the governor of California, he lost two bids to be the Republican presidential nominee, but won the nomination and then the presidency in 1980. Reagan instituted a policy of supply-side economics, also dubbed "Reaganomics," which lowered taxes to encourage investment in business and economic growth. He also lowered government spending (although his administration later raised taxes on several occasions). After several years of continued recession, the U.S. economy rebounded. His presidency saw the weakening of the Soviet Union and Communism throughout Eastern Europe.

## REMBRANDT VAN RIJN (1606–1669)

Dutch painter considered one of the best European artists of all time. He was the leading painter of the Dutch Golden Age. He began his career as a portrait painter but painted many biblical scenes, relying on Dutch Jews for inspiration for the subjects of his paintings. He also painted portraits of friends and many self-portraits. In the later years of his life, he experienced financial hardship and was buried in an unmarked grave.

## ROBINSON, JACKIE (1919–1972)

One of the first African-American baseball players to play in the major leagues. He played first base for the Brooklyn Dodgers in 1947, making the Dodgers the first team to play a black man since the 1880s. He won the Rookie of the Year award that year. Robinson played ten seasons, was in six World Series, and played in six All-Star games. In 1997 major league baseball retired his jersey number, 42, from all teams.

## ROOSEVELT, FRANKLIN DELANO (FDR) (1882–1945)

Thirty-second president of the United States (1933–1945). He served four terms, the only president to do so. He oversaw the country's response to the Great Depression and entry into World War II after the Japanese attack on Pearl Harbor, an event he referred to as "a day that will live in infamy." He was a progressive politician, raising taxes under his New Deal Coalition and beginning programs such as Social Security.

## ROOSEVELT, THEODORE (1858–1919)

Twenty-sixth president of the United States (1901–1909). He is considered the father of the progressive movement, which aims to increase the size and scope of government to provide more benefits and advantages to citizens from the lower classes. His public persona was built around his adventures as a soldier, hunter, and explorer. He was forty-two when he became president, making him the youngest man to serve in that office.

## SANDBURG, CARL (1878–1967)

American writer and poet, famous for his biography of Abraham Lincoln. He worked as a reporter for the *Chicago Daily News* and wrote a series of children's stories or American fairy tales to match the experience of American children. His biography of Lincoln won the Pulitzer Prize.

## SHAKESPEARE, WILLIAM (1564–1616)

English playwright. His known works include 154 sonnets and thirty-eight plays, considered to be among the greatest works of literature ever produced. Shakespeare was also an actor and part owner of the acting group, the Lord Chamberlain's Men. His first works were mostly comedies, but as he matured as a writer and actor he wrote tragedies and historical plays, as well as plays that have no clear classification. Many details of his personal life are unknown, which has led to much speculation about him, including whether he really wrote the plays that were published under his name.

## SHAW, GEORGE BERNARD (1856–1950)

Irish literary critic, novelist, and playwright. He wrote more than sixty plays. Many of his plays are comedies, but they also address social ills. He was a self-proclaimed socialist and spoke out on working conditions and other liberal issues. He was awarded the 1925 Nobel Prize in literature.

## STEINEM, GLORIA (1934–)

American feminist and activist who became a leading figure of the women's movement in the late 1960s and 1970s. Her support of abortion rights helped her to gain national media attention. She started *Ms.* magazine to create a voice for feminist-leaning women.

## STEWART, JIMMY (1908–1997)

American actor who won one Academy Award and was nominated for five more. Known for his distinct voice and gestures, he tended to play loveable, wise characters in such movies as *Harvey* and *It's a Wonderful Life*. In addition to acting, he had a distinguished military career, rising to the rank of brigadier general in the U.S. Air Force Reserve. He served in World War II as a pilot and remained active in the reserve into the Cold War. He seldom spoke of his military service.

## TCHAIKOVSKY, PYOTR (1840–1893)

First Russian composer to achieve international success. He wrote symphonies, operas, and ballets, and traveled and conducted throughout Europe and finally New York City in the United States. Tchaikovsky studied for a career as a civil servant. Although he was musically inclined, there was little opportunity for him to study music until he enrolled in the Saint Petersburg Conservatory. Initially, Russian music critics offered mixed reviews of his compositions because they lacked traditional Russian musical elements, but his music gained in popularity among the common people and then spread to Europe.

## TRUMAN, HARRY S. (1884–1972)

Thirty-third president of the United States (1945–1953). Serving as President Franklin D. Roosevelt's vice president, Truman became president upon Roosevelt's death in 1945. To end the war with Japan, Truman sanctioned the first— and only—use of nuclear weapons. Although he was initially a popular president for overseeing the end of World War II and the return of U.S. soldiers to their homes, he was only narrowly re-elected in 1948. He proclaimed the Truman Doctrine to contain communism internationally.

## VAN GOGH, VINCENT (1853–1890)

Dutch postimpressionist painter whose influence was felt by many modern painters. He was prolific, completing more than 2,100 works of art notable for their strong brushwork and vibrant colors. He suffered from mental illness and extreme anxiety about his ability as an artist. He died at thirty-seven from a gunshot wound that many believed to have been self-inflicted, although a gun was never found.

## VIVALDI, ANTONIO (1678–1741)

Italian composer and violinist born in Venice. Also a Catholic priest, he was a baroque composer, writing mostly violin concertos, though he also wrote more than forty operas. His most popular composition is titled *The Four Seasons*, a group of violin concertos. His music increased in popularity in the twentieth century.

## WALLACE, GEORGE (1919–1998)

Southern politician embroiled in racial controversies. He served as governor of Alabama and ran for the presidency four times, losing each time. Throughout his political career he was an ardent segregationist, but eventually he reversed his position, stating that he did not wish to meet his Maker with unforgiven sin. An assassination attempt in 1972 left him paralyzed.

## WARREN, EARL (1891–1974)

A chief justice of the United States. He is credited with building the power of the Supreme Court to a more level playing field with Congress, as stated in the U.S. Constitution. The Warren Court ended racial segregation of public schools and ended public and school prayers. He was the head of the Warren Commission, which conducted the official investigation into President John F. Kennedy's assassination.

## WASHINGTON, BOOKER T. (1856–1915)

African-American educator and author. During the late nineteenth century, many of the southern states had taken away the rights of blacks through disfranchisement laws. Washington fought against these laws and discrimination by working with influential whites and blacks. He also consulted with numerous Republican lawmakers and with Presidents Theodore Roosevelt and William Howard Taft.

## WASHINGTON, GEORGE (1731–1799)

Father of the United States and its first president. During the Revolutionary War, he led the Continental Army against the British. After the war, he presided over the convention that created the U.S. Constitution. He served two terms as president and when asked to serve a third term remarked that he did not want to appear as the nation's king. Before joining the revolutionary cause, Washington was a surveyor and solider.

## WELLES, ORSON (1915–1985)

American actor, writer, and director. He did groundbreaking work in radio, theater, and movies. His radio production of *War of the Worlds* in 1938 was so realistic that people tuning into the program believed it to be a newscast and that aliens were invading the country. His film *Citizen Kane* (1941) is considered one of the greatest movies of all time. Later in his career he made such movies as *The Magnificent Andersons* (1942) and *Macbeth* (1948).

# WILSON, WOODROW (1856–1924)

Twenty-eighth president of the United States (1913 to 1921). Along with Theodore Roosevelt, he was a leader of the progressive movement. When running for his first term, he stated that he was against the United States entering World War I, though after he was elected he propelled the country into the war. He participated in the Versailles Conference, which drew up the terms for ending the war and proposed establishing a League of Nations. He also instituted the first federal income tax. Prior to serving as president, he was the governor of New Jersey and president of Princeton University.

# WRIGHT, FRANK LLOYD (1867–1959)

Credited by the American Institute of Architects as being "the greatest American architect of all time." He designed more than 1,000 buildings and oversaw the construction of 500 more, including such classics as Fallingwater in Pennsylvania and Robie House in Chicago. He believed in what he termed "organic architecture" in which the building is designed to be in harmony with the spirit of the environment where it is to be built.

# ZEITGEIST

Popular trends in a culture characterized by a particular time period; for example, the Roaring Twenties, 1960s flower power, and 1980s, the decade of greed. Zeitgeist, a German term meaning "the spirit of the age," can influence writers, composers, and thinkers of a generation and the influence of that time period will be expressed in their work.

# 6 THINGS YOU SHOULD KNOW ABOUT POLITICS

**66** It is enough that the people know there was an election. The people who cast the votes decide nothing. The people who count the votes decide everything. **99**

—Joseph Stalin

In this chapter you'll learn the 100 things you need to know about politics from the earliest autocracies to the new political movements in the twenty-first century. You will learn how banana republics are countries in which foreign interests control the natural resources of these nations for their own benefit with little or no concern for the people. How the domino theory was invoked by American policymakers to justify intervention in Southeast Asia. How the Geneva Convention outlines the humane treatment of prisoners of war and is universally accepted by virtually all nations. How political machines use patronage to control voters. The essentials you need to know about politics are right here.

## ABSOLUTE MONARCHY

A system of government in which a monarch holds unrestricted political power over the people. A limited monarchy has some form of checks and balances such as a constitution. Monarchies are generally passed from father to son based upon primogeniture (though this is not always the case). Saudi Arabia and Qatar are current absolute monarchies.

## AD HOMINEM

An argument made against a person's character and/or intelligence, and not his or her ideas. An ad hominem attack aims to strike down a person's credibility or to discredit him or her personally. Ad hominem arguments are logical fallacies, or errors in reasoning. However, they are very effective—and common—in politics.

## AD NAUSEAM

When a point is made repeatedly, well after the audience understands, and to listen further becomes nearly sickening.

## APARTHEID

A system of racial segregation of blacks in South Africa that lasted from 1948 to 1994. The segregation was enforced by the government of the National Party of South Africa and started after World War II, but was condemned in 1966 by the United Nations. The 1948 legislation classified people in four categories—native, white, colored, and Asian—and created segregated residential areas. Apartheid was resisted through demonstrations, violence, and trade embargoes. In the 1990s President Frederick Willem de Klerk (1936–) began to end apartheid.

## APPROPRIATIONS

The process by which the U.S. Congress or state legislatures authorize payments for spending measures; also known as the power of the purse. Money is appropriated for special projects or uses, such as funding schools and welfare programs, building roads, and bridges, and so on. Congress and state legislatures have appropriation powers while the judicial and executive branches of government have no such authority.

## ARAB-ISRAELI CONFLICT

Tensions between Arabs and Israelis over land rights and positions of borders within Palestine and Israel. The United Nations voted Israel into membership in the late 1940s. However, the Palestinians have continued to protest what they view as an expropriation of their land. Tensions between Egypt, Syria, Jordan, and Lebanon on one hand and Israel on the other have been the cause of wars and terrorist attacks.

## AUTOCRACY

Similar to a monarchy or dictatorship, an autocracy is a governmental system in which one person or group holds unlimited control and authority over the government; also known as unrestricted authority over a group of people.

## BALANCE OF POWER

Nations, though possessing varying amounts of power and resources, can balance one another in order to maintain relative stability in the world. The balance of power ensures that a single nation cannot dominate all other nations. Because of national pride, political leaders want to strengthen their nations' standing in the world; therefore, the leading nations will all be strong nations. The balance of power between these countries assures there will be no reason for war.

# BALANCE OF TERROR

Referring to a situation in which a number of nations possess nuclear weapons. No nation will attack any other nations because of the threat of global nuclear war. For example, during the Cold War the United States and the Soviet Union maintained a balance of terror even as both nations mounted an arms race.

# BALKANIZATION

To divide a nation or region into smaller areas, usually leading to circumstances in which each new state is hostile to its neighbors. Balkanization usually makes such states politically ineffectual. The term comes from the 1920s when the Balkan Peninsula, formerly controlled by the Ottoman Empire, was divided into small warring nations.

# BANANA REPUBLICS

A derogatory term referring to the politically unstable nations in Central America whose economies are propped up by foreign interests; small tropical countries in the West with economies built on tourism and the export of fruits. Therefore, they are called "banana republics." The foreign interests control these nations for their own benefit with little or no concern for the people in these countries who are often exploited and underpaid.

# CAPITALISM

An economic system in which private citizens own property, with access to natural resources to manufacture goods and provide services. Adam Smith, in his 1776 book *Wealth of Nations,* expressed his belief that people seeking their own economic self-interest benefit society more than if they tried to aid society directly. Even when an individual selfishly pursues wealth and personal enrichment, many other people are benefited.

## CAPITAL OFFENSE

In the justice system of a nation, an offense meriting the death penalty. These offenses usually include murder and, in some cases, treason against the government and its constitution. The word "capital" comes from the Latin word *caput,* meaning "head." Capital punishment formerly referred to execution by beheading.

## CAUCUS

Political meeting. A caucus can be held among people of the same political affiliation to discuss positions on issues, select candidates to seek office, plan political rallies, etc. Within a political party, factions within the party meet to discuss strategies to gain favor for their sides on particular issues. For example, there is the Black Caucus in the U.S. House of Representatives that discusses issues relative to African Americans.

## CHECKS AND BALANCES

In a republic form of government, the power of the legislative, judicial, and executive branches to void, amend, or otherwise control the actions of one another. The system was created by the Founding Fathers to protect against one branch of government's obtaining absolute power. Under the U.S. Constitution, both the House of Representatives and the Senate must vote on measures for them to become laws. Even then the president can veto the law, but the law can still be upheld if a two-thirds majority of the House of Representatives and Senate vote in its favor.

## CIVIL DISOBEDIENCE

Refusing to obey society's rules or laws to make a political or social point. Nonviolent means of raising awareness of an issue. Gandhi fasted for many days to rally his countrymen in India's campaign to win its independence from the British. To fight against racial discrimination in the United States in the 1960s, the civil rights leader Martin Luther King Jr. encouraged movements of civil disobedience including sit-ins and protests.

# CLEAR AND PRESENT DANGER

A phrase made famous by Supreme Court Justice Oliver Wendell Holmes Jr. Holmes argued that even though freedom of speech is guaranteed by the First Amendment, it can be limited in order to protect the public. For example, a person does not have a constitutional right to yell, "Fire!" in a crowded theater when there is no fire. This creates, in Holmes's words, a "clear and present danger" to the public at large.

# CLOTURE

A vote taken by a legislative body to end debate on an issue; a tactic employed by a political party to force immediate action and a vote on a motion. It comes from the French word for "the action of closing."

# COALITION

A group formed by people with common interests. Alliances created of groups with similar needs and goals; such groups combine resources in pursuit of those goals. In nations with multiple political parties, coalitions are formed around issues, and compromises are made to get legislation passed.

# COMMUNISM

Government and political system that aims to create a classless society in which the people share common ownership of a country's natural resources and means of production. Communist ideas were expounded by many thinkers, many of whom argued that a gradual political shift will occur wherein countries' governments will become more and more socialistic, and eventually become communistic. At the beginning of the twentieth century, after the Russian Revolution, the Soviet Union spread Communist ideology through Eastern European countries. Later in the 1940s, China became a Communist country and remains so today.

# CONFEDERATION

An alliance between independent groups or states, which maintain a large degree of autonomy. In the United States, the thirteen colonies initially formed a confederation after the Revolution, which eventually gave way to a new country under the Constitution. Canada is a confederation of provinces, and the Swiss cantons form the oldest known confederation.

# CONFLICT OF INTEREST

When a person in a position of influence must act in an official capacity that could benefit him personally. A conflict between a person's public obligations and private interests. For example, if a congressional representative votes on a piece of legislation, and the result of that vote impacts her business holdings in a positive way, she is guilty of a conflict of interest. To avoid conflicts of interest, people may recuse themselves from voting or acting on certain matters.

# CONSENT OF THE GOVERNED

In a democracy, the principle that the voice of people should determine who is elected to public office and thereby have a say in the destiny of the affairs of their nation. This notion emerged in the eighteenth century as new ideas of democracy flourished across Europe and in America. The Declaration of Independence sets forth the principles of consent of the governed.

# CONSERVATISM

The desire to minimize government and maximize individual freedom. In the United States, the conservatives promote restoration and preservation of what they view as the principles in the original Constitution of limited government. Historically, conservatives have also opposed changes in social mores.

# CONSTITUTION

In politics, a document setting forth the system of principles that constitute a government's belief and practices; a document that contains, in written form, the principles and laws of the government. The U.S. Constitution was enacted in America in 1789.

# CONSTITUTIONAL MONARCHY

Monarchical government in which the sovereign exercises limited control; when a monarch rules with a constitution in place that limits his or her powers; also, in absence of a formal constitution, when a monarch rules and is bound by customs and laws of the country. Throughout history, nations with kings and queens have ranged from absolute monarchies to constitutional monarchies.

# CONTAINMENT

United States policy in the twentieth century to limit Communism to the Soviet Union, Eastern Europe, Korea, and China. A number of presidents cited the policy of containment as the basis for their actions taken toward the Soviets including U.S. intervention in the Korean and Vietnam wars. The policy of containment fell out of favor during the Nixon administration, which attempted to open diplomatic doors to the Soviet Union and China.

# COUNTERINSURGENCY

Fighting rebel forces that threaten to bring down the established government; the effort to counterattack efforts of subversive groups to bring down the government by guerrilla warfare. Extensive counterinsurgency tactics were first developed by the U.S. military during the Vietnam War.

# COUP D'ETAT

In politics, quick and swift action by a small group to take charge of the government, usually by force or threat of force. Occasionally, this can refer to a parliamentary maneuver by one party to take over the government or it can mean the overthrow or seizure of power by an outside political group. A coup d'etat usually does not have mass support. Because the takeover is by a small group, the general population may first hear about it from the new rebel government.

# CULTURAL IMPERIALISM

The penetration of a weaker nation's culture by that of a stronger nation. Also known as the cultural impact of imperialism. The extensive spread of American culture after World War II is an example; today, almost every country in the world contains McDonald's outlets.

# DARK HORSE

In politics, a surprise candidate for office; when a political candidate reveals few details about himself or herself. A dark horse is someone unknown or unexpected, who often emerges as a top contender to win the race. In 1831 the word appeared in a novel by Benjamin Disraeli (1804–1881), *The Young Duke*, in which an unknown horse wins a race.

# DEFICIT

When more money is owed by a government than can be covered with tax revenues. A deficit is not a debt. Deficits occur when government spending is greater than the revenue it collects, usually through taxes or transfer payments. The total deficit is the primary deficit plus interest payments owed on the nation's debt. Governments operate under deficits because economies go through cycles of high unemployment in which tax revenues decrease and low unemployment in which tax revenues increase. As tax revenues increase, the government is able to reduce its deficits.

## DEMAGOGUE

A political leader known for flashy rhetoric used to arouse the emotions of constituents. The term originated in ancient Greece, where it referred simply to a leader of the people. Today, it means a person whose speaking ability, often using false arguments, helps to sway public opinion to his or her side of the issue. Demagoguery has a negative connotation, applied to political leaders who distort issues and lie to win over the people.

## DEMOCRACY

Government of the people by the people; government officials are elected by the vote of the people; a form of representational government in which elected officials are vested with rights from constituents to represent their interests. The United States is a democratic republic. The term also refers to the idea of equal rights for all citizens under the law.

## DEVELOPING NATION

Typically, a nation whose economic systems are still in the process of evolving. In such nations, farming is usually the main source of wealth, and manufacturing industry is weak or nonexistent. There is little modern innovation in any of a developing nation's industries.

## DICTATORSHIP

A government in which all power is wielded by one person, the dictator; governing without the consent of the governed or absolute control by one person. The dictator is not responsible to the people by election for his or her power, but rather has ended all opposition and quells any challenges. The most infamous dictator in modern world history is Adolf Hitler.

# DIPLOMACY

The act of negotiating relationships between nations. Each nation has a corps of diplomats stationed around the world who engage in discussions about how the countries can work together to promote their common good. Diplomacy involves negotiation regarding economic and political matters, and can also involve talks on disarmament, human rights, or environmental issues.

# DIPLOMATIC IMMUNITY

Privileges of diplomats and their staffs while living abroad and representing their governments in official capacities. As foreign nationals, they and their families are exempt from the laws of the land. They cannot be arrested or taxed, searched, or have their property seized by the country in which they are residing. When a diplomat from a foreign country is threatened with arrest or search and seizure, she can claim diplomatic immunity.

# DISFRANCHISEMENT

To divest a person of the right to vote; in another sense, to render a person's vote ineffective or less effective. Disfranchisement occurs when governments make it difficult for certain less-advantaged groups in a nation to vote or when a political group intimidates voters and implies negative consequences for voting.

# DOLLAR DIPLOMACY

When a government, through diplomatic or military efforts, works to implement policies in foreign lands that promote the business interests of private citizens of the country. Also, a nation's foreign policy designed to ensure increased wealth for investments in foreign countries or in global financial markets.

# DOMINO THEORY

The idea that if one nation falls prey to conquest by a stronger nation, its neighbors will also be eventually conquered. The domino theory was conceived in the United States to describe the Soviet Union's expansionist desires to spread Communism worldwide and was used to justify U.S. involvement in Southeast Asia. The argument was made that eastern European countries fell one after another under Communist rule, just like dominos.

# EQUAL OPPORTUNITY

In the United States, government policies enacted to protect people's rights not to be discriminated against in the workplace on account of race, gender, age, or physical limitations. An equal opportunity employer is in compliance with equal opportunity laws.

# EQUAL PROTECTION OF THE LAW

The Fourteenth Amendment to the Constitution requires states to guarantee the same rights, privileges, and protections to all citizens. The amendment requires states to enforce laws equally and not discriminate when creating or enforcing future laws. The amendment was ratified in 1868 as part of Reconstruction after the Civil War.

# EQUAL TIME

In the United States, rules regarding radio and television airtime. In the 1960s the Federal Communications Commission required radio and television stations, in order to receive a license to broadcast, to give equal time to responsible opposing viewpoints. The equal-time provisions applied to political campaigns and public issues. In the case of a political candidate, the radio or television station was required to offer the opposing candidate free or paid use based on what had been given to his or her opponent. The provision is no longer U.S. policy.

# ESCALATION

In politics, to put added pressure on an opponent in war or in foreign relations. In war, a policy of escalation means to step up military campaigns through aggressive action. The desired goal is to increase the pace of the war to ensure enemy defeat. In foreign relations, a policy of escalation means to offer a nation a one-time agreement that can be pulled off the table if it is not immediately accepted.

# EXPATRIATION

To exile a person from his or her country; to take away citizenship. An expatriate can also refer to someone who voluntarily resides in another country for an extended period of time. Expatriation is derived from the French word *expatrier,* meaning "to banish." After World War I, Ernest Hemingway (1899–1961), James Baldwin (1924–1987), Gertrude Stein (1874–1946), and other artists and writers from the United States lived as expatriates in Paris.

# FACTION

A smaller group within a larger group. In politics, a small group united around an issue. For example, the NAACP was a faction within the larger civil rights movement, pushing for reforms to U.S. government policy on race relations. Factions can also refer to groups within political parties; for instance, the Tea Party is a faction on the right wing of the Republican Party.

# FAVORITE SON

In politics, a candidate nominated for national office who is from the state in which the nominating convention is taking place. Sometimes the term refers to a politician who is liked in his or her own home state, but not popular outside it. Favorite sons are sometimes nominated early in the process of choosing a candidate, either as a courtesy or to give them some leverage later in the nomination.

# FIRST-STRIKE CAPABILITY

In nuclear war, the ability to conduct a first or surprise attack of overpowering force with the objective of destroying as many of the enemy's nuclear weapons as possible. The intent of first-strike capability is to weaken the enemy nation's retaliatory attack. The United States sought to maintain first-strike capability against the Soviet Union during the Cold War.

# FRANCHISE

The rights granted by a government to its citizens to vote for representation. Originally in the United States the rights of franchise were only afforded to property owners. Gradually, the Constitution was amended to make it unconstitutional for the states or federal government to deny franchise, or voting rights, based on skin color—though this right was only fully enforced as a result of the civil rights movement in the 1960s. Women were guaranteed the right to vote in 1920.

# FREEDOM OF ASSEMBLY

Under the First Amendment to the U.S. Constitution, the right of American citizens to hold public meetings and form groups without government interference. The First Amendment states that people have the right to peaceably assemble. Freedom of assembly allows like-minded people to come together to promote ideas and issues important to them. Freedom of association is sometimes included with freedom of assembly.

# FREEDOM OF ASSOCIATION

Under the First Amendment to the U.S. Constitution, the rights of like-minded people to form groups to express opinions or dissent from government policies. The Constitution guarantees this right without government interference.

# FREEDOM OF THE PRESS

Under the First Amendment to the U.S. Constitution, the right to publish materials without government interference. In a free and open society, the freedom of the press allows people to publish opinions and ideas, which permits the free flow of ideas and information. There are still laws dealing with publishing obscenity, libel, defamation, etc., though these are far looser in the United States than in many other countries. It is the responsibility of the citizens to support only those media outlets they deem appropriate and factual.

# FREEDOM OF RELIGION

Under the First Amendment to the U.S. Constitution, the right to worship (or not worship) without government coercion. The Founding Fathers of the U.S. Constitution did not want the government to sanction an official state religion such as the Church of England. Rather they wanted to ensure that people were free to worship according to the dictates of their individual consciences.

# FREEDOM OF SPEECH

Under the First Amendment to the U.S. Constitution, the right to voice one's opinion without government censorship or interference. The rights of the people to express opinions in the public square. There are some restrictions on freedom of speech (see "Clear and Present Danger"), but in general, apart from libel and defamation, virtually any speech is permitted.

# GENEVA CONVENTION

International rules outlining the humane treatment of prisoners of war. These were created in 1864 in Geneva, Switzerland, and are almost universally accepted. The convention also addresses treatment of the wounded and dead in war, as well as civilians, and contains rules prohibiting attacks upon hospitals and ambulances.

## GENOCIDE

The conscious policy of elimination directed against a particular ethnic group. Genocide is usually conducted under the pretense of war. The extermination is sometimes motivated by the wish to possess the lands of the group (for example, the policy followed by the American government toward Native Americans in the nineteenth century) and sometimes based on ideology (as was the case with Nazi policy toward the Jews).

## GLASNOST

In the late 1980s, a time of new openness in the Soviet Union when government officials began to discuss issues relating to the Soviet economy and its geopolitical status in the world. During glasnost the Soviet government for the first time permitted some criticism of the government. Soviet Premier Mikhail Gorbachev (1931–) led glasnost, first mentioning it in a speech in 1985. The term "glasnost" was first used by Vladimir Lenin. Several years after glasnost, the Soviet Union collapsed largely due to the arms race with the United States.

## GLOBAL VILLAGE

A term that originated in the late 1960s to describe how the world was becoming increasingly connected through technology; shrinking by coming closer. Increasingly, through interdependent relationships, the world has turned into one global village. Scholar Marshall McLuhan (1911–1980) originated the term, describing how the world would, over time, become more and more interdependent as nations cooperated on political issues in their best interests.

# GREATEST GOOD FOR THE GREATEST NUMBER

Also known as utilitarianism, which holds that the proper course to follow is to maximize the utility of providing the greatest degree of happiness for as many people as possible. It can be argued that the objective of democratic governments is to provide the best life opportunities for the greatest number of its citizens. In a world of limited resources, so the argument goes, no government system is able to provide the greatest good for *all* of its citizens.

# GUERRILLA WARFARE

Warfare carried out by small bands of irregular troops against an established army. Guerrilla warfare is unconventional warfare using surprise and destructive attacks not only against the standing army, but against buildings and landmarks; its aim is to send a political message to the people and the government. Guerrilla warfare has been common in South America, where local bands of citizens seek to rise up against oppressive or colonialist governments. It was also practiced by the Vietnamese against the United States in the 1960s and 1970s. The term "guerrilla" comes the Spanish word *guerra*, for "war."

# HABEAS CORPUS

When a person is accused of a crime, he or she must be brought before a judge to determine if there are grounds for the arrest and detention. The judge must determine if the charges presented before the court justify charging the defendant or holding him or her in jail. The purpose of habeas corpus is to ensure that a person is not illegally imprisoned prior to the court date, which could impede the defendant's ability to prepare a rebuttal to the charges.

# HUMAN RIGHTS

The concept that every person has the basic right to be free to work and pursue his or her path in life. Governments should not take away or interfere with these basic rights. Human rights are considered universal and form the basis for much international law. After World War II, the United Nations General Assembly, motivated by the horrors of the Holocaust, drafted the *Declaration of Human Rights*, which spells out these rights in some detail.

# INTERNATIONAL LAW

Legal rules by which nations agree to work together and accept as binding in international matters. Many of the decisions regarding international law are determined by the World Court in the Hague in the Netherlands. International law serves as the basis or agreed-upon foundation by which nations conduct international relations.

# IRON CURTAIN

The invisible barrier between West and East during the Cold War. The West represented the ideals of freedom, while the East represented the tightly controlled Communist governments. The Iron Curtain was effectively torn aside with the fall of the Berlin Wall in 1989. England's prime minister Winston Churchill (1874–1965) coined the term "Iron Curtain" in 1946 in a speech in Fullerton, Missouri.

# LEFT WING

Liberal or progressive movements. Leftists believe that government should provide more for the people and control economic growth. They are also proponents of redistribution of wealth throughout society. They pursue government programs that will create greater equality among all classes of society.

## MANDATE

The authority given a politician or political body to enact legislation based on wide public support. For example, when a president is re-elected by a wide margin of votes, she can claim that the public supports the platform she ran on and, therefore, Congress should go along with legislation supporting her agenda.

## MASSIVE RETALIATION

In military strategy or foreign relations, the threat of launching nuclear weapons. In the Cold War, the United States and the Soviet Union maintained an uneasy peace out of fear that if one attacked the other, it would suffer a massive retaliation. A balance or sorts was achieved because of the threat of nuclear devastation.

## MONARCHY

A system of government in which the king or queen holds all power. In a monarchy, all ruling authority is handed down through hereditary lines. There have been limited monarchies, in which the sovereign and a parliamentary body shared power, and absolute monarchies, where the king alone wielded all power.

## MORATORIUM

A period of delay; when a nation agrees to halt activity for a certain length of time. In the recent past this has referred to nuclear weapons. For periods, the United States and Russia have agreed to a moratorium on developing and deploying nuclear weapons.

## NATIONAL LIBERATION MOVEMENTS

Struggle, usually military, by a third-world country to free itself from the rule of a colonial power. Such movements are called wars or revolutions of national liberation. Oftentimes, those fighting for their freedom employ guerrilla warfare tactics.

## NATURAL RIGHTS

Rights of people that arise from the natural law; in politics, the idea that people have basic rights given to all humans by God who created them. These rights, because they are God-given or arise from the natural state of the world, cannot be taken away by a government, and governments should exist and operate within the framework of these natural rights. The Declaration of Independence states that natural rights include life, liberty, and the pursuit of happiness.

## NEMESIS

In politics, an opponent on a bill or issue; in Greek mythology, the goddess of retribution and vengeance. A nemesis refers to someone or something that is difficult to overcome or conquer. At her sanctuary, Nemesis descends as the spirit of divine retribution to put those who display pride and arrogance (hubris) before the gods.

## NOBLESSE OBLIGE

The obligation of people from royal or noble families, or powerful social positions, to act with honor and generosity, both to one another and to the masses. The French phrase means "nobility obliges." Today, the phrase is often used condescendingly, poking fun at people who feel superior to others based on their social status or wealth.

## NONALIGNED NATIONS

Nations that do not support or align themselves with or against the main superpowers in the world. In the recent past, this meant nations that were not allies of the United States or the Soviet Union. Today, the Non-Aligned Movement includes 120 member countries. The idea for the organization came in 1961 from Josip Broz Tito (1892–1980), the Yugoslavian president who had broken with Stalin. The Non-Aligned Movement allowed countries in developing parts of the world to stay outside the arms race between the United States and the Soviet Union.

# NONVIOLENT RESISTANCE

Making political statements through nonviolent means of protest, such as public gatherings, economic boycotts, etc., in order to raise awareness of issues and effect change. Nonviolent resistance movements are designed to seek attention from media and politicians in order to influence public opinion, gaining sympathy for their causes. Sometimes nonviolent resistance involves breaking laws, which results in arrests and prosecution, also raising awareness of the cause.

# OLIGARCHY

Government by the few; a structure where all power is held by a few people or a group of people. Usually oligarchies are ruled by the wealthy people of the nation, a royal family, or a few military leaders. An oligarchy can also refer to a small group of people who wield strong influence on government procedures.

# PASSIVE RESISTANCE

Showing dissent from government policies through peaceful methods of protest marches, boycotts, etc. The most famous example of passive resistance is Mohandas Gandhi (1869–1948), whose fasting and marches helped free the Indian nation from British rule. He strongly opposed violent revolution and was horrified by the wave of violence that accompanied Indian independence in 1947.

# PEACEFUL COEXISTENCE

Policy of maintaining peace between nations with different ideologies. Usually refers to relations between the United States and the former Soviet Union. The government of the Soviet Union under Stalin maintained an official policy of peaceful coexistence, arguing that the Communist countries could exist alongside capitalist countries. This contradicted previous Soviet ideas that Communist and capitalists countries could never exist side by side. Peaceful coexistence became the centerpiece of Soviet policy for much of its existence.

## PLUTOCRACY

Governmental rule by the wealthy and powerful; when a wealthy class of people rules. The power and ability to govern comes from wealth, and because of wealth this class of people feels it is best suited to rule. The term is often used in a pejorative sense. Plutocracies have included the Roman Republic, ancient Greece, and Japan prior to World War II.

## POLARIZATION

The separation of people and their increased alienation from one another based on beliefs, values, and opinions; a situation in which people's opinions align around extremes. As people become polarized over issues, their leaders must search for compromise, or gridlock will develop.

## POLITICAL MACHINE

A group of people who control a political party either at a national or local level; a political group that seeks to control, usually through patronage, the functioning of a political party and through it, the government.

## PRE-EMPTIVE STRIKE

A swift and surprise attack before an enemy can attack. When intelligence reports demonstrate a likelihood of an enemy attack on a nation, the nation may best be served by attacking first to prevent the attack or, through the might of its force, intimidate the military force of the potential attacker. Often a pre-emptive strike is a show of force to prevent the outbreak of a real war.

## PROPAGANDA

Misinformation spread by a government to gain public or world support. Propaganda can also be used to denigrate a group of people or an opposing political force. Propaganda is sometimes true but often only half-true or altogether false. The aim of propaganda is not to tell the truth, but to sway public opinion.

# RAPPROCHEMENT

In politics, a reconciliation followed by new mutually beneficial relationships. To follow a policy of rapprochement is to rebuild and reconcile once-broken relationships. These may involve trade or political relations and their rebuilding may allow nations to work together for peace and other worthwhile causes.

# REALPOLITIK

A German word meaning the "politics of reality." To base government policy on what provides true political power for a nation. Realpolitik implies political conduct that is realistic rather than ideal or moral. Such policies build international relations based on terms that are best for their country, and show little or no concern for other nations.

# REFERENDUM

A vote by the citizens on measures affecting them, as opposed to a vote by elected officials. For example, many state taxes have been subject to referenda. They are usually restricted to state, county, or city measures. A referendum is put on a ballot after a group of citizens articulates the issue and then secures a large number of signatures of citizens who want to vote on it.

# REPARATIONS

Monetary compensation for wrongs or injustices. In war, reparations are often paid by the defeated country to the conquering nations. After World War II, Germany paid reparations to the Jews. Native Americans have been paid reparations from the U.S. government for illegal land acquisitions from tribal nations. Some civil rights leaders have called upon the U.S. government to pay African Americans reparations for injustices inflicted by slaveholders.

# REPUBLIC

A government that functions under a constitution and in which people vote officials into office; government by the people for the people. A republic is an agreement by citizens to abide by a constitution and to elect representatives to represent their interests. The United States is a democratic republic.

# RIGHT WING

Conservative movement, or right-leaning wing of the Republican Party. Traditionally, conservative or right-wing groups support cutting government spending and limited government power. They have also generally opposed certain social issues such as the right to abortion, recognition of gay marriage, and removing religion from public life. Right-wing adherents generally believe in the ability of the individual to make correct choices without government mandates.

# SANCTIONS

Penalty levied against a nation for violation of international laws or standards. For example, a country vigorously pursuing nuclear capabilities could be subject to sanctions imposed by other nations. Sanctions can take the form of extremely high tariffs, refusal to trade in certain goods, etc. Sanctions are used by the international community as a way to move rogue nations toward peace.

# SEDITION

Rebellion against the government; inciting other people to harm or rebel against the government; to commit treason or incite an insurrection. Calling for rebellion or government overthrow in a speech or book is considered seditious, as is taking direct action to cause harm to a government institution.

## SOLIDARITY

Unity among a group of people involved in a common cause. Solidarity was the name of a Polish labor union movement in the 1980s that increased its ranks to several million workers. The Solidarity movement is credited with bringing down the Communist government of Poland.

## SOVEREIGNTY

A government's authority and right to rule within its own borders. A government will not accept, generally, extra-national restrictions on its authority. Governments assume they have to rule according to their own authority.

## STRAW MAN

An insubstantial idea that is easy to debate and pick apart. A rhetorical tactic, by which you attribute a weak argument to your opponent—not necessarily one that he's making—and destroy it. A straw man is often used in debate as a way to draw attention away from the real issue.

## SUFFRAGE

The right to vote in public elections. In the United States in the early twentieth century, women fought for the right to vote. They launched a suffragist movement that held mass demonstrations across the country. The Nineteenth Amendment to the Constitution, stating that states could not deny the right to vote based on gender, was ratified in 1920.

## THIRD WORLD

Poverty-stricken nations in Latin America, Central America, southern Asia, and Africa. People in third-world countries generally subsist through primitive farming methods. These countries are also characterized by limited technology and manufacturing capabilities.

## ULTIMATUM

In political negotiation (or, for that matter, in any other kind of negotiation), the final offer or demand. If the ultimatum is not met, there will be, it is implied, serious consequences. In international politics, rejection of an ultimatum might result in a declaration of war, sanctions, or trade embargoes.

## WELFARE STATE

A state in which the government provides financial aid and other benefits to lower-income citizens in the form of housing, food, clothing, etc. Government programs in the United States include food stamps, Social Security, and unemployment insurance. Many welfare states are based on the political ideas of redistribution of wealth through high taxation of wealthy citizens. The wealth passes from the highly successful people in society through the government to the lower-income citizens in the form of benefits and government programs.

## ZERO-SUM GAME

In game theory, a situation in which the sum of wins and losses equals zero; also, where the sum of all winnings by all players is zero, so no one is declared the winner. In politics, when trade-offs between various parties involved in negotiations balance one another in their effect. Therefore, no one has "won" the negotiation.

# 7
## THINGS
### YOU SHOULD
### KNOW ABOUT
## SCIENCE &
## TECHNOLOGY

66 The saddest aspect of life right now is that science gathers knowledge faster than society gathers wisdom. 99

—Isaac Asimov

**I**n this chapter you'll learn the 100 things you need to know about science and technology from the great mind of Archimedes to natural selection to astrophysics. You will learn that when a subatomic particle collides with its antiparticle, both particles are annihilated in a puff of energy. How entropy leads to the inevitable disorganization of closed systems. How genetic engineering can manipulate the DNA material within cells to correct genetic defects or improve plants and animal breeds. How quantum mechanics burrows into the world of the very small with strange particles such as positrons and quarks. Prepare to have your mind stimulated.

# ABSOLUTE ZERO

The temperature at which molecular activity in a substance ceases; temperature of negative 273 degrees Celsius. The faster the molecules move in a substance, the hotter the substance. At negative 273 degrees Celsius the molecules have no kinetic energy and produce no heat.

# ADAPTION

State or act of adapting as in evolutionary processes. This is a key element of natural selection. In biology, an alteration in an organism by which it improves its chances for propagation. Some creatures can change in their environment such as a species of birds whose feathers gradually change colors to blend into their natural surroundings so as to protect the birds from predators.

# AEROBIC

Organism requiring oxygen for life and growth. Aerobic respiration is the process by which cells use oxygen to survive in their environment. Aerobic exercise—running, cycling, etc., for extended time periods—increases the heart rate so the body requires more oxygen.

# ALPHA RADIATION

Alpha particles released from radioactive isotopes. Alpha particles are made up of two neutrons and two protons and are produced in the process of alpha decay. Alpha particles are positively charged.

# ANAEROBIC

In the absence of oxygen; living without air. For example, fermentation is a process in which oxygen is not required. An anaerobic organism is any living thing that does not require oxygen to live—for instance, single-cell microbes such as bacteria. The term was coined by Louis Pasteur from the Greek prefix *an*, meaning "without"; *aer*, meaning "air"; and *bios*, meaning "life."

# ANTIPARTICLE

A class of subatomic particles; in physics, a particle whose properties have the same mass but the opposite charge of a specific elementary particle. For example, the positron is the antiparticle of the electron. When a particle collides with its antiparticle, both are annihilated and produce other particles.

# APOGEE

In astronomy, the farthest point from the earth in an object's orbit; as a metaphor, the highest point or climax; also, the most distant point. Relative to the earth, apogee refers to when the moon or a satellite is in its farthest point away from the earth.

# ARCHIMEDES (ca. 287 B.C.E.–ca. 212 B.C.E.)

Greek mathematician and physicist who discovered specific gravity; regarded as one of the greatest ancient scientists. He discovered hydrostatics and invented the lever. He designed the first siege engine to break apart city walls in warfare, and the screw pump, which pulls water from low-lying areas into irrigation ditches.

# ASEXUAL REPRODUCTION

Reproduction that does not involve the union of male and female sexual reproductive cells (such as when a sperm and egg merge to create a new cell to form a new organism); reproduction of single-cell organisms through the process of fission—a division into two or more equal parts from a plant that develops into new cells. Spores and other plantlike organisms can multiply by asexual reproduction.

## ASTROPHYSICS

The branch of science that studies the physics and chemistry of planets, suns, systems of stars, and galaxies. Astrophysicists study how matter and radiation in the interiors of planets, suns, and stars interact. Astrophysicists also examine the motions of various celestial bodies, how much light they emit, the mass of stars, their motion in the universe, and similar questions.

## ATOMIC NUMBER

The number of electrons gathered around an atom's nucleus; also the number of protons, or positive charges, in the nucleus of a particular atom. The atomic number determines the position of the element on the periodic table.

## ATOMIC WEIGHT

Weight of an atom; ratio of the average mass of an atom to one-twelfth the weight of the carbon-12 atom. The periodic table includes atomic weights of all the elements.

## ATROPHY

Wasting away of the human body or part of the body; to decrease in size or degenerate. For example, patients' muscles can often atrophy after many weeks of bed rest unless they are regularly exercised. In medicine, the term refers to the death and reabsorption of cells.

## BACONIAN METHOD

Method of scientific experimentation made famous by Sir Francis Bacon (1561–1626). Bacon emphasized that one should draw conclusions from observed and recorded facts. Bacon explained his method in his book entitled *Novum Organum* (The New Method), published in 1620. He put forward his ideas on scientific investigation in response to Aristotle's *Organon*, which teaches the principles of logic. The Baconian method is the foundation for modern-day scientific discoveries through identifying a problem, gathering data, and testing hypotheses.

# BALANCE OF NATURE

When an equilibrium in the population of animals and plants in an ecosystem is achieved through the interdependence of the organisms; the stable state of natural communities. The idea holds that as one species is impacted in the environment, there is a ripple effect through the whole ecosystem.

# BETA RADIATION

Beta particles undergoing radioactive decay. These are high-energy electrons or positrons emitted by certain radioactive nuclei. These high-energy electrons have a negative charge. Beta particles are used in treating eye and bone cancer.

# BIG BANG THEORY

The idea that the universe was created billions of years ago after a sudden massive expansion from a singularity. Suns, stars, and planets were formed as this expansion continued—in fact, the expansion is still continuing. This theory is supported both by the laws of physics and by observations that galaxies are traveling away from one another. The big bang theory is widely accepted by scientists as the explanation of the origin of the universe.

# CELL DIFFERENTIATION

The process by which less-developed cells become more developed. As human, animal, and plant cells increase in complexity, they grow from a single-cell zygote to multicellular types. Cell differentiation changes the cell's metabolism, functions, and communications signaling, size, and shape. These changes are directed by gene expression. "Dedifferentiation" is the opposite of cell differentiation; it occurs when more-developed cells become less developed.

## CENTER OF GRAVITY

The point on a surface where a single force can be applied to equally balance the surface of an object; also known as the center of mass of an object; the center of mass of an object in a gravitational field when balanced.

## CHEMICAL EQUILIBRIUM

A state of balance in chemical reactions; in chemical reactions when substances break down at a similar rate. The term can also mean the point at which the number of molecules in substances becomes constant and when chemical reactions proceed at equal rates.

## CHEMICAL EVOLUTION

The theory that during the earth's earliest history, complex organic molecules evolved from simpler inorganic molecules. Scientists believe that inorganic materials were deposited into the earth's oceans when meteorites crashed into the earth. Evolutionists argue this is the first phase of life developing on this planet. Some have speculated that this period lasted as long as one billion years.

## CONVECTION

When heat is transferred through a substance by movement or circulation of currents from another region. For example, in the case of boiling water, heat originates on a stovetop, then moves to the water in the pot, and then into the air. Conduction is when heat is transferred through a liquid or gas by motion of hotter materials into a cooler region.

## CROSS-FERTILIZATION

In biology, when an organism is fertilized by the union of an egg from a female with a sperm from a male. In botany, cross-fertilization refers to when the ovum of a plant is fertilized by the stamen of another plant. In the social sciences, when two groups, disciplines, or cultures exchange ideas and knowledge to the benefit of both parties, they cross-fertilize.

## DIFFRACTION

Phenomenon that occurs as light and sound waves move through and around obstacles. As the waves diffract, their energy is changed. Diffraction is the bending of light and sound waves as well, and describes how the waves spread through openings in surfaces.

## DOMINANT TRAIT

In genetics, an allele of a gene that masks the expression of another allele in the same gene. The practical upshot of this is that certain alleles tend to be expressed more frequently. For example, if a green-eyed person and a brown-eyed person have a child, chances are greater that the child will have brown eyes, because the allele for brown eyes is dominant.

## ECOLOGICAL NICHE

A "space" within the ecological environment in which a certain organism or group of organisms can thrive; also, the role that a plant or animal plays in its environment that allows the organism and the other species in the environment to exist. Different plants and animals may vie for the same role or niche in their ecological environment. In this competition, the more-dominant plant or animal will win the role and fill the niche.

## ELECTROMAGNETIC SPECTRUM

The complete range of all electromagnetic radiation; a continuum of all magnetic and electric radiation. The spectrum goes from gamma rays, small amounts of radiation, and high frequencies at one end to long waves (radio waves), a great deal of radiation, and low frequencies at the other end. Visible light rests near the center of the electromagnetic spectrum.

# ELEMENTARY PARTICLES

The particles that make an atom. How many of these are there is an ongoing question. Electrons, protons, and neutrons have been identified. Today, scientists believe that protons and neutrons, which make up the atom's nucleus, are made of even more elementary particles called quarks. Particle accelerators are being developed that dramatically increase the speed and energy of atomic particles and direct them into collisions, breaking them down into still smaller components to further study their properties.

# ENTROPY

The tendency of a closed system to evolve toward a state of disorder; a law of thermodynamics that the energy of a system tends to dissipate. A closed system evolves toward a state of entropy because no new energy is being introduced into it. In sociology, entropy refers to the decline of a society or culture.

# EQUILIBRIUM

In physics, the state of balance between two opposing forces, which cancels each other out. In politics and social organizations, equilibrium refers to the balance of power and influence to keep things equal, when all influences cancel each other out to create a balanced situation. In chemistry, the term means the state at which reactants and products no longer change over time.

# ESCAPE VELOCITY

In astrophysics, the speed necessary for an object to escape the gravitational pull of a larger object; the minimum speed that a planet or star, near a larger planet or star, is moving so that it will continue to move away from the larger planet or star instead of being pulled by gravitational force into an orbit around it. The escape velocity of the earth is approximately 11.2 kilometers per second, and the escape velocity of the moon is approximately 2.4 kilometers per second. The escape velocity for a celestial body near a black hole must be faster than the speed of light, and since nothing can exceed the speed of light, nothing can escape the gravitational pull of a black hole.

# EUGENICS

The belief that life conditions for the general population can be improved by limiting reproduction of people with genetic defects, such as mental and physical handicaps. Positive eugenics refers to encouraging reproduction by people considered to have positive inheritable characteristics. Negative eugenics is when reproduction is discouraged for people considered to have negative inheritable characteristics. The term was coined in 1883 by English scientist Francis Galton from the Greek word *eugenes*, meaning "of good stock" or "well-born." Advocates of birth control employed eugenics as an argument in the early twentieth century in the United States. Hitler and his regime also used it in Nazi Germany.

# EXOTHERMIC

Chemical change that releases heat; a chemical reaction that releases energy from a system in the form of heat. At the simplest level, burning wood in a fire produces an exothermic reaction in which heat is released. An exothermic reaction can also release energy in light form such as an explosion or flame. A battery works by an exothermic reaction that releases electricity. Endothermic, which means "absorption of heat," is the opposite.

## EXPANDING UNIVERSE

In astrophysics, the idea that everything in the universe is moving away from the center and therefore the universe is expanding in size. This theory is based on observations through space of red shifts in faraway galaxies. These galaxies appear to be receding from other galaxies. This theory is related to the big bang theory.

## FLASH POINT

In chemistry, the lowest temperature at which the vapor above a liquid will ignite and produce a flame. The flash point is usually lower than the temperature necessary for the liquid itself to ignite. Metaphorically, the point at which a critical event occurs that causes an additional significant event.

## FORCE

In physics, the influence that causes a change in something—either from a state of rest to a state of motion, or in its form. Force causes a body to change speed and movement. The amount of force is measured in a vector quantity of magnitude and direction. The mass is multiplied by the acceleration of the object, and the net force is the sum of the measurements of all given forces on an object. Natural forces include gravity, the electromagnetic force, the weak nuclear force, and the strong nuclear force.

## GAMMA RADIATION

A photon with electromagnetic radiation from a decaying atomic nucleus. Energy of a gamma ray can range from 10,000 to 10 million electron volts. Gamma radiation is the most powerful radiation in the electromagnetic spectrum.

# GENERAL THEORY OF RELATIVITY

In physics, a theory originated by Albert Einstein (1879–1955) in 1916; the central argument is that gravity is related to the curvature of space-time. Gravity affects both space and time as well as matter. This is one of Einstein's two theories of relativity. The *special* theory of relativity holds that there can be no speed of motion greater than the speed of light, and that time is relative and dependent on the motion and location of the person measuring time. The theory also holds that as velocity increases, mass also increases.

# GENETIC ENGINEERING

Manipulation of genes in order to change hereditary traits in humans, animals, or plants; redirection of the DNA material within cells to correct genetic defects or improve plants and animal breeds. Using biotechnology, genes can be cloned to produce new traits and then inserted into cells. Genes can also be deleted from cells. Genetic engineering is widely used in agriculture, medicine, and biotechnology.

# GEOMETRIC PROGRESSION

In mathematics, a sequence of numbers in which each number is created by multiplying the previous number in the chain by a constant. For example, if five as the constant is multiplied by one, equaling five, and then five is multiplied by five, equaling twenty-five, the following geometric progression is created: 1, 5, 25, 125, 625, and so on.

# GEOPHYSICS

In geology, the study of the physics and movements of the earth. The field covers such areas as seismology, oceanography, meteorology, geomagnetism, etc. Geophysicists study how the earth's physical properties interact below the earth's surface from its core to its tallest mountains. The study of geophysics also deals with the earth's relationship to other planets—for example, how the moon controls tidal movements.

# GRADUALISM

Pursuing a larger goal through small, gradual steps. Instead of pushing for change quickly, someone who believes in gradualism will launch a series of events that will gradually bring about the desired goal. In geology, gradualism includes the idea that the current appearance of the planet is the result of subtle changes over vast amounts of time. The opposite is catastrophism, which holds that the earth was formed through sudden violent events that effected massive change on a large scale.

# GRAVITATION

Force of attraction between two objects. Sir Issac Newton (1642–1727) theorized gravitational attraction is a function of objects' mass and distance. In physics, Albert Einstein described gravitation in his general theory of relativity in the context of space-time. He posited that gravity warps space-time, governing the motion of objects.

# HALF-LIFE

The amount of time it takes for one-half of the atoms of a radioactive substance to decay. The half-life of something does not indicate that one-half of its life has diminished. The half-life of the nuclei gives a good indication of when the object started to decay. It's the foundation of radiocarbon dating, one of the most reliable methods of dating objects of a great age. In pharmacology, also known as the amount of time it takes for the activity of a drug to lose one-half of its effect in the body.

# HEAT CAPACITY

In science, the heat required to raise a substance or object's temperature by one degree. Depending on the substance or object being heated, greater or lesser amounts of heat are required to increase the temperature by one degree.

# HEISENBERG UNCERTAINTY PRINCIPLE

In physics, the idea that in a quantum mechanical system, position and momentum cannot be accurately measured at the same time because measuring one will affect the other. The principle is named after Werner Heisenberg (1901–1976) who first postulated the theory.

# HOMEOSTASIS

Tendency of a living system to maintain its balance and stability. When a situation arises that would disturb the natural balance and stability of an organism, the organism's many parts work together in a coordinated effort to repel the threat and regain balance and stability. In the human body, when you get too hot, you sweat, cooling your skin; when you get too cold, you shiver to raise your body heat. In sociology, the tendency for disturbances or outside threats introduced into the social order to be dealt with so balance of the group can be regained.

# HORSEPOWER

The measurement required to lift 33,000 pounds one foot in the air in one minute; 550 foot-pounds per second of force. This comes out to about 1.5 times more power than that exerted by a strong horse. Today, horsepower is primarily used to describe the power of car engines. In an informal use of the word, it can refer to anything with great force or power.

# HYBRIDIZATION

By crossbreeding, manipulating genes to produce animals or plants with specific characteristics. It's a method used widely in agriculture to produce food with more nutrients or better taste, or in the production of animals with desirable qualities for food. Hybridization is also used to refer to the result of groups coming together to form a better group by merging their best qualities or to refer to two elements of something coming together.

# HYPOTHESIS

A set of propositions designed to explain something that is capable of being tested and disproved; an explanation put forth to explain a certain observable phenomenon. The hypothesis is then tested to determine if there is evidence that supports it or contradicts it. A hypothesis is the beginning point for scientific inquiry. To test a hypothesis, data is gathered and the hypothesis is empirically tested.

# INERTIA

Resistance to movement; inactivity; slow and difficult motion; sluggishness. In physics, the term describes how when an object is at rest, it will remain at rest until acted upon by an outside force. At that point it will travel along a straight line until another external force acts upon it. Inertia is the tendency of matter or physical objects to resist action or movement.

# INORGANIC CHEMISTRY

Study of noncarbon-based compounds. Inorganic compounds are those compounds not biological in origin. These compounds do not contain hydrogen and carbon bonds. Organic chemistry deals with chemical reactions that involve carbon, the element on which all living matter is based. There is much overlap between inorganic and organic chemistry.

# INORGANIC MOLECULES

Molecules not found in living things. However, inorganic molecules are widely prevalent throughout the natural environments of the earth. Inorganic molecules may contain carbon. Although diamonds are composed of carbon atoms, they are inorganic because diamonds are considered minerals and not a biological composition.

# IONIZATION

The process of converting molecules into ions by adding or removing charged particles. By removing electrons or ions, the chemical structure of the molecule's electrical charge is changed. The term also means to form ions from molecules through a chemical reaction by introducing an increased temperature or contact by an electrical discharge or radiation. For example, when an electron attached to a molecule is forced to absorb a given amount of energy it breaks the bond to the molecule and is free to move about, changing the properties and structure of the original molecule.

# KINEMATICS

The geometry of motion; describes the motion, or direction, of a moving object without attention to the cause of the motion. Kinematics studies linear movements, or trajectories, as well as acceleration and velocity. In astrophysics, kinematics describes the motion of the stars and planets.

# KINETIC ENERGY

Energy of a system when it is in motion. The kinetic energy equals the force required to bring the object to rest. Kinetic energy is equal to one-half the mass of the body times the square of its speed. Kinetic energy relates to potential energy that can be released, such as a charged battery, an avalanche poised to fall down the mountainside, or water behind a dam.

# LATENT HEAT

As a substance changes to a different state, it releases or absorbs latent heat—for example, when water freezes and becomes ice or ice melts and becomes liquid water. Thunderstorms are created when the air absorbs latent heat from water vapor in the atmosphere. Latent heat is radiated or absorbed at a constant temperature and pressure.

## LINEAR MOMENTUM

Product of mass times the velocity of an object. A car moving at 60 miles per hour requires a great deal of force to get it moving at that speed, and it requires a great deal of force to get the car to stop. If the car were smaller and moving at 20 miles per hour, it would require less linear momentum to reach that speed as well as to bring it to a stop.

## LOCUS

A location or locality; a place where something is located or an event has occurred. "Locus of control" is the center place for a group of activities or power center. In genetics, the term refers to the position of a gene on a chromosome; in geometry, it means the center of the points that form certain geometric shapes.

## MAGNETISM

In physics, the effect of a magnetic field upon matter; when a magnetic field is created by a moving electric charge. Magnetic fields are established when electric charges are in motion, meaning that electrons are moving around the nucleus of an atom. Charged lines come together and create the north and south poles of the magnet.

## MALIGNANT

Harmful; tending to produce death; also cancerous, characterized by uncontrolled growth of the cancer cells. Malignant cancer cells are invasive and tend to metastasize. When a tumor is benign, it does not threaten the health of a person.

# MELTING POINT

Temperature at which a solid will turn into liquid form; the opposite of freezing point. The melting point of ice is 32 degrees Fahrenheit (likewise, water's freezing point is 32 degrees Fahrenheit). Melting point is affected by the purity of the material's composition as well as the atmospheric pressure.

# METABOLISM

Processes in living organisms by which growth is sustained, energy is made available, and waste is eliminated; processes in a living organism necessary for life. Through metabolism, chemical substances are broken down and synthesized and distributed through the organism.

# METAMORPHOSIS

Changes in a living organism from stage to stage in its life development. A classic example is the transformation of a caterpillar to pupa to adult butterfly. Metamorphosis is also applied to a change in form or structure, such as when a tadpole experiences the metamorphosis into a frog. The term is used commonly to explain major changes in an object.

# MITOSIS

Typical method of cell division. The nucleus divides into two new nuclei, each containing the same number of chromosomes as the parent nucleus. Before mitosis occurs, each chromosome is copied to form two chromatids, identical strands of genetic material. The chromosomes attach to the cell spindle at the center of the cell. The chromatids split off to the opposite end of the cell. A membrane forms around each of the two groups of chromosomes and then divides, and a nucleus is created.

# MUTATION

Change or alteration in the nature or form of something; in biology, a genetic or chromosomal change from the parent model in one or more of the characteristics or traits. In conception, if a change takes place in the sexual reproductive cells, mutations can occur that will alter the development and/or structure of the offspring. Mutation is any sudden changes in the nucleotide sequence, reinterpretation of the DNA coding, or a physical rearrangement of the chromosome.

# NATURAL SELECTION

Evolutionary process by which life forms that are able to adapt to their environment will have the better odds of survival and propagation. Species that are better able to survive in their environment tend to reproduce in greater numbers, passing to their offspring the favorable traits that aided in the parents' survival. Species less well adapted to their environments tend to die out.

# NEWTON'S LAW OF MOTION

One of Sir Isaac Newton's three laws of classical mechanics. The first law of motion is that a body will remain at rest or in motion with constant velocity unless an outside force acts upon it. The second law is that the sum of the forces acting on a body is equal to the product of the mass of the body times the acceleration produced by the forces, with motion in the direction of the forces. The third law of motion is that for every force acting on a body, the body exerts a force having equal magnitude and the opposite direction along the same line of action as the original force.

## NORMAL DISTRIBUTION CURVE

In statistics, the bell-shaped curve that shows the expected rate of results. Experiments usually show near the average, but will sometimes deviate. The narrower the bell curve the more confidence you can have in the experiment's results. The mathematician Abraham de Moivre (1667–1754) discovered the "normal curve" in 1733.

## NUCLEAR FISSION

Splitting apart of an atomic nucleus into nuclei of lighter atoms with a resultant release of energy. Fission is the scientific basis of nuclear weapons such as the atomic bomb and the hydrogen bomb. In biology, fission refers to asexual reproduction when a single-cell organism divides into two independent cells.

## NUCLEAR FUSION

When two atoms are fused together, releasing energy. The nuclear reaction when nuclei of lighter atoms are formed, or are fused together to form the nuclei of heavier atoms, results in massive energy output. Stars, including the sun, are powered by the fusion of hydrogen atoms. Heat forces the nuclei to collide at high speeds and a chain reaction is created.

## ORDER OF MAGNITUDE

A rough estimate of the importance or magnitude of something; order of something measured by the power of ten.

## OSMOSIS

The process of absorbing something gradually; passage of molecules through a membrane until the molecules are evenly distributed to both sides of the membrane. Osmosis sometimes refers to people's ability to learn by gradual, almost unconscious, acceptance of ideas.

## OXIDATION

Process by which deposits form on metal surfaces as they are exposed to the elements. In chemistry, when a substance is exposed to oxygen and the atoms in the substance lose electrons and the valence, the strength of chemical bonding of the substance, is increased.

## PARTICLE ACCELERATOR

High-tech machinery that propels and accelerates charged molecular particles at very high speeds and energies. Particle accelerators, also called synchrotrons and synchrocyclotrons, produce collisions of particles. The results of these collisions are analyzed, and physicists develop theories of molecular chemistry and physics.

## PHASES OF MATTER

The forms of matter: gas, liquid, or solid. Matter passes through phases based on environmental change such as temperature changes. Freezing involves moving from a liquid to a solid. Melting involves moving from a solid to a liquid form. Evaporation involves moving from a liquid to a gas.

## PLANCK'S CONSTANT

In physics, the basic physical constant at the heart of quantum mechanics. Max Planck (1858–1947) discovered in 1900 that light was emitted in small "packets," called quanta. Planck's constant can be used to calculate the energy of each quantum.

## POLARIZATION

Division into two opposite sides or factions; in physics, when rays of light have different properties as they spread in different directions; the separation of positive and negative electric charges. In biology, the term refers to differences between two points in living tissues, such as inside and outside the cell wall.

## POTENTIAL ENERGY

The energy of a system, such as a charged battery. In physics, the potential energy of a system is based on the position of the subatomic particles that make up the system, as well as magnetic or gravitational fields around it. It is not the motion of the system as it moves; rather, it is the possible energy that can be released by the system.

## PROBABILITY

The possibility of something occurring. Probability is based on the ratio of the actual event occurring to the total number of possible occurrences of that event. For example, if you roll a six-sided dice, the likelihood, or probability, of rolling a "three" is one in six or 1:6. In statistics, it is the measure of confidence you can have that an event will happen.

## PYTHAGOREAN THEOREM

A mathematical equation for determining the length of the hypotenuse, or longest side, of a right-angle triangle. $A_2 + B_2 = C_2$ where C is the length of the hypotenuse, and A and B are the lengths of the other two sides. So if one side, A, of the right triangle is 3 feet long and another side, B, is 4 feet long, $3_2$ (9) $4_2$ (16) = $5_2$ (25). Therefore, the length of the hypotenuse is 5 feet.

## QUANTUM LEAP

A sudden change in the nature of a thing; abrupt change in a system as it moves from one state to another state. In physics, the term means when an electron, atom, or other particle moves out of its orbit, changing the energy of the system. A major advancement in something or a new finding in a field can also be called a quantum leap.

## QUANTUM MECHANICS

In physics, the study of subatomic particles. Quantum mechanics was first developed in an effort to understand how light could behave both like a wave and like a particle. The solution, that light exists in packets, called quanta, and the subsequent development of the principles of quantum mechanics was the work of such physicists as Max Planck, Niels Bohr (1885–1962), Werner Heisenberg, and Erwin Schrödinger (1887–1961).

## REDUCTION

In biology, the situation when the number of chromosomes is reduced by half when a cell divides as in the process of meiosis; in chemistry, when an atom gains electrons and experiences a decrease in valence. Valence is the capacity of an atom to take on or give up electrons and thereby change its structure and physical properties.

## REFRACTION

The bending of light, sound, or heat waves; in physics, the change in wave velocity of light, sound, or heat waves as they are forced to pass from one medium to another; refraction of light as through lenses or a prism.

## RELATIVITY

Albert Einstein's theory that space and time are relative and not absolute concepts. The *special* theory of relativity holds that nothing can exceed the speed of light, time is relative and dependent on the motion and location of the person measuring time, and as velocity increases mass also increases. The general theory of relativity holds that gravity affects the curvature of space-time as well as governing the motion of objects.

## SCIENTIFIC METHOD

Method of scientific experimentation that emphasizes drawing conclusions and testing theories based on observation. Scientists identify a problem, gather data, and empirically test a hypothesis. The intent is to discover and demonstrate scientific truths with research that can be repeated by other groups of scientists. Replicating the results in different experiments strengthens the foundation of the theory.

## SOCIOBIOLOGY

The belief that social norms are the result of evolutionary change. Its most important proponent is Edward O. Wilson (1929–). The theory has been strongly critiqued by many evolutionary biologists.

## *SPECIAL* THEORY OF RELATIVITY

In physics, Albert Einstein's theory that nothing can exceed the speed of light. The theory also holds that time is relative and depends on the motion and location of the person measuring time. For instance, if one twin were to travel to a star in a spaceship moving at close to the speed of light, when she returned she would discover that her twin had aged more than she had.

## SPECIES

Biological classification; group of animals with common characteristics and genetic traits that set them apart from other groups. In biology, determining factors of species classification include if the members of the species resemble one another and are able to breed among themselves and not with another group or species.

## SPECIFIC GRAVITY

Ratio of density of a substance to the density of a similar standard substance. For liquids, the density of water is considered the standard substance to which all other liquids are compared. For gases, hydrogen is considered the standard substance to which all other gases are compared.

## SPEED OF LIGHT

The speed that light can travel in a vacuum has been calculated as 186,000 miles per second. By light traveling in a vacuum, Einstein meant that the light travels unimpeded by objects. As light passes through objects, it slows slightly. He estimated that light can travel more than 5 trillion miles in one year, a distance known as one light-year.

## STANDARD DEVIATION

In statistics, after data has been collected from research, the standard deviation measures how much of the data or research findings fall around the mean as portrayed in a bell curve. A high standard deviation means that the data is widely scattered along the bell curve. A low standard deviation means that the data lie close to the mean, which is the center of the bell curve.

## STATISTICAL SIGNIFICANCE

The probability that research results could have happened by chance and not the cause and effect studied in the research. The statistical significance is determined by a numeric value known as the margin of error. After statistical significance has been determined, the research study can claim to be accurate with, for example, a 5 percent margin of error. Or, for instance, we can say that we have a 95 percent confidence level that the study measures what it claims to have studied.

# SUPERCONDUCTIVITY

When metals can conduct an electric current with almost no resistance. In physics, almost-perfect conductivity in materials is reached at absolute zero. Scientists believe that materials that can be heated to temperatures several hundreds of degrees above absolute zero may provide new, state-of-the-art developments for producing electrical energy.

# THERMODYNAMICS

The study of how temperature impacts the properties of a mechanical system. The conversion of heat and mechanical energy into one or the other, or different forms of energy. The law of thermodynamics states that the total energy of a system cannot change; heat will not flow from a cold to a hot object without something to make it flow; in a mechanical system, it is impossible to produce the temperature of absolute zero.

# TITRATION

In chemistry, the process to determine what is required to convert a material or substance into another form. A titration is done by adding a liquid agent of a particular strength and volume in different amounts to a material or substance until the desired chemical reaction is achieved.

# TWIN PARADOX

From Albert Einstein's theory of relativity. Einstein posited that if one identical twin remained on earth (an inertial system), and the other twin traveled through space at the speed of light in a spaceship for a long time and returned to earth, that the space-traveling twin would be younger than his brother. This phenomenon of time dilation at high speeds has been demonstrated scientifically with atomic clocks.

## VAPORIZATION

Change of a liquid into a vapor or gaseous state, as, for instance, when water changes into steam; when a liquid changes form through vaporization, such as when increasing heat turns a liquid substance into a gas.

## VISCOSITY

In chemistry, how the molecules in a fluid resist movement and, therefore, the speed at which the liquid can flow.

# THINGS
## YOU SHOULD
## KNOW ABOUT THE
# SOCIAL
# SCIENCES

**66** Believe that life is worth living and your belief will help create the fact. **99**

—William James

In this chapter you'll learn the 100 things you need to know about the social sciences from Freud's id, ego, and superego to ethnocentrism to the effects of sensory deprivation. You will learn how an alter ego is an alternate personality. How developmental psychology studies changes in behavior in the different stages of life from infancy to adulthood. How introverts and extroverts react differently in social situations. How the nature vs. nurture debate among sociologists concerns how much an individual's personality is shaped by his or her environment or heredity. How the psyche has come to be known as the center of a person's consciousness. From Freud to Skinner, it's all here.

## ACCULTURATION

To take on the social and cultural values, ideas, and traits of another group. For example, when immigrants come to a new country, they transition into the new culture by adapting to a new language, customs, and social mores. Another term for acculturation is assimilation. Acculturation can also refer to when two different groups merge and elements of both groups' cultures merge, or one culture dominates the other. When a person merges into a new culture there are often visible changes—for instance, as she adopts clothing styles of the new group.

## ALIENATION

Being cast out or shunned by a person's culture or peer group; the condition of being an outsider. Alienation is typical among minorities and other groups with limited resources and power. In psychology, when a person's emotions are held back so he feels disconnected from himself and the external world. In another sense, when changes occur in society and new elements of the culture dominate, some people accustomed to the old way of life will feel alienation.

## ALTER EGO

Another side to a person, usually showing a different side of his personality. Latin for "another I." When it is discovered that someone has led a double life, it is said that she had an alter ego. Sometimes refers to a close friend possessing a similar personality to your own and an uncanny ability to think like you.

## ANIMISM

The belief that natural objects in the world possess souls that animate their being; the idea that natural objects have a spirit essence separate from their physical body. Animism applies to more than just humans and animals; it can refer to mountains, rivers, rocks, and more.

## ANTI-SEMITISM

Discrimination, hostility, and/or hatred toward people of Jewish heritage. Anti-Semitism ranges from silent discrimination against individual Jews to programs of mass extinction or persecution such as the Holocaust during World War II, the Spanish Inquisition against the *conversos* (converted Jews), and the Cossack massacres of Jews in the Ukraine.

## ANXIETY

Feelings of stress or apprehensiveness. Butterflies in the stomach. Heightened levels of awareness and physical arousal. People feel anxiety in new or stressful situations. Anxiety can be a warning sign of psychological danger or a threatening situation.

## ARCHETYPE

The first or primal form of something. The model or pattern from which other things are copied; a repeated symbol in art. In psychology, the idea propagated by Carl Jung (1875–1961) that every person has certain unconscious ideas or mental images in their psyche, which represent symbols universal to humankind. These symbols appear in dreams and are recurring themes in fairy tales and mythology. Archetypes can include the hero, the martyr, the wise old man or wise old woman, the damsel in distress, the child, etc.

## ASSIMILATION

When an individual or group accepts the cultural norms and traits of another group; similar to acculturation. The individual or group is said to have assimilated into the new group. As a verb, assimilate means to learn new information or absorb, as in digestion, into the body, or it can mean to take on the social and cultural values, ideas, and traits of another group.

# ATTACHMENT

Part of the bonding process between a child and parents; the psychology of making connections to other human beings. Sadly, when a child has not properly attached to a loving adult figure, the child is maladjusted to his environment and his behavior will reflect this lack.

# BEHAVIOR MODIFICATION

Psychological learning techniques intended to change a person's behavior. These techniques can include positive reinforcement, aversion therapy, and biofeedback. The goal is to teach new skills or change undesired behavior. The new behavior is reinforced by rewards and punishments. Aversion therapy means providing unpleasant conditions as a consequence of a particular behavior, motivating the subject to change her behavior pattern. Biofeedback involves monitoring the body's physical responses (brain activity, muscle tension, blood pressure, etc.) to different situations.

# BEHAVIORISM

Psychological theory that behavior of humans and animals is best studied by direct observation of their behavior. Other psychology theories focus on mental states or inner drives and those motivations for behavior. Behaviorists such as B. F. Skinner (1904–1990) complained that these theories were based on speculation on the happenings of the inner world of an individual. Skinner and other behaviorists argued that mental states are best studied by observing changes in behavior caused by certain stimuli.

# BLACKBALL

To exclude a person or group; to cast a vote against someone—for example, against their membership in an organization. To decide against as a job applicant or reject someone from membership in a private club or organization such as a fraternity is to blackball him. Originally, secret ballots were conducted by dropping white or black balls into a sealed box—hence, the origin of the term.

## BLACKLIST

To shun, ban, or ostracize; a list of people or organizations under suspicion or disfavor. For example, political groups often maintain lists of organizations with ideals counter to the groups' agendas and strategize on how best to halt the effectiveness of those organizations. Companies sometimes blacklist former employees thought to be disloyal or dishonest.

## CASTE

A social hierarchy. Each caste has its place in the society and, as a result, accompanying privileges and obligations. Caste is inherited, and people are generally permitted to marry only within their own caste. It is very difficult to move up to a higher group in the caste system.

## CLASS CONSCIOUSNESS

The awareness by someone of his or her economic and social status. In Marxist terms, the degree to which a member of the working class is aware of her oppression by capitalism. Awareness that society is divided into classes and how these classes relate to each other based on social position and economic advantages indicates class consciousness.

## CLASS STRUGGLE

Conflict between different economic classes in a society. When the poor are pitted against the rich in their struggle to achieve a higher level of existence. This idea is attributed to Karl Marx, who defined class struggle as the tensions and conflicts between capitalists, who own the means of production and natural resources, and the workers, who sell their labor power to the capitalists. Marx theorized that the conflict between the capitalists, whom he termed the bourgeoisie, and the workers, whom he called the proletariat, will result in socialism overtaking capitalism as the world's dominant ruling political system. Class struggle is also sometimes characterized as class war.

# COLLECTIVE UNCONSCIOUS

The unconscious ideas that all people have in common; psychologist Carl Jung's theory that humankind shares a common mythic understanding of human existence that resides in the unconscious mind. The collective unconscious contains mythical symbols as well as instincts and collective memories of humanity. This unconscious knowledge of ancestral experience manifests itself through dream states, fairy tales, and mythology.

# COMPULSION

When a single thought takes over the possession of a person's mind. Compulsions can be relatively harmless or, in an extreme state, result in pathological behavior. For example, someone who has an obsession with germs on his hands will compulsively wash his hands to get rid of the object of the obsession—in this case, germs.

# CONDITIONED RESPONSE

In behavioral psychology, a predictable, learned response to a stimulus. Ivan Pavlov (1849–1936), the Russian physiologist, conducted a series of famous experiments in which he was able to train dogs to salivate when a bell rang. At first he presented the dogs with meat at the ringing of a bell. Over time, the dogs became conditioned to expect food whenever the bell sounded. Finally, they salivated from hearing the bell alone.

# CONSPICUOUS CONSUMPTION

Spending lots of money to impress people with one's wealth; buying expensive and unnecessary items or purchasing luxury goods to display one's economic purchasing power. Conspicuous consumers do so to attain or maintain a particular social status. Sociologist and economist Thorstein Veblen (1857–1929) invented the term to describe this trait in his book *The Theory of the Leisure Class*.

# COSMOLOGY

In astronomy, the study of the origin and structure of the universe and humanity's place in it. Cosmologists theorize about first causes, time and space, human freedom, evolution, etc. Throughout world history, both primitive and modern humans have pondered the cosmos and their place in its vastness. There are many myths and legends among primitive cultures explaining the existence of humans.

# COUNTERCULTURE

Culture created by those who reject the values and opinions of society; fringe or alternative culture to the mainstream. The counterculture that emerged in the 1960s in the United States was a rejection of American middle-class values. The term was coined by Theodore Roszak (1933–2011) in his book *The Making of a Counter Culture*.

# DEFENSE MECHANISM

In psychology, an unconscious process of the mind that protects a person from painful and uncomfortable thoughts, desires, or impulses. The mind may, for example, block a memory of an unpleasant event. Rationalizing that a certain behavior or thought pattern is acceptable is another defense mechanism, as is repressing unacceptable thoughts or feelings. In the body, a defense mechanism refers to the means by which cells eradicate other cells that could induce illness.

# DEMOGRAPHY

Study of population statistics. A demographer looks at the size and structures of populations, including such things as birth rates, marriages, family size, death rates, social impacts, diseases, etc. The word originated around 1880 and comes from the Greek word *demos*, meaning "people."

# DEVELOPMENTAL PSYCHOLOGY

School of psychology that studies the psychological life span of individuals from birth to death. Developmental psychologists look at changes in behavior in the different stages of life from infancy to childhood to adolescence, adulthood through midlife to old age, and finally death. They study cognitive development, social and emotional development, and how people transition through the different stages of life.

# EGO

One of the three basic parts of Freud's model of the mind. The ego moderates between the id and superego, maintaining a balance between the pleasure seeking of the id and the order-seeking superego. The superego, in general, represents a person's desire to live an upstanding, appropriate life. The id represents a person's desires for pleasure.

# EGOCENTRIC

When a person considers himself or herself as the most important thing. An egocentric person has little interest in the concerns or wishes of others. In another sense, the word is used to convey the idea that a person considers things primarily in relation to himself or herself.

# EGOTISM

To be extremely self-centered and preoccupied with oneself. Excessive feelings of self-importance. "Egoism" is a philosophical term used to describe the feelings of importance one has in relation to other things in the world and universe. In its pathological form, extreme egotism can become narcissism, which takes self-absorption to a higher level. Narcissism derives its name from Narcissus, a character from Greek mythology who fell in love with his own reflection and could not bear to look away.

## ETHNOCENTRISM

In sociology, the belief that a culture, social group, or racial group is superior to other cultures, social groups, or racial groups; dislike of other groups or cultures. The term was coined by William Sumner (1840–1910) who defined it as "the technical name for the view of things in which one's own group is the center of everything, and all others are scaled and rated with reference to it."

## ETHNOLOGY

The study of cultures to understand their structures in terms of politics, language, mythology, or history. In anthropology, a term referring to the study of the historical development of cultures, including their origins and impact on humankind and societies as a whole. To gather information, ethnologists sometimes live among the races they are studying. Ethnology includes research into the differences and similarities among races and their relationships to other races.

## EXPATRIATION

An action to deprive a person of citizenship. It can also refer to a person living for an extended period of time in a country different from that in which she is a citizen. An "expat" refers to a person who is temporarily without citizenship status, or residing permanently in another country different from his upbringing. During the twentieth century, many American writers and artists—including James Baldwin (1924–1987), Ernest Hemingway, and Josephine Baker (1906–1075)—were expats in France. In Nazi Germany, during World War II, the German government expatriated many of its liberal citizens, including Albert Einstein and Thomas Mann.

## EXTROVERSION

Personality trait in which a person enjoys engagement with other people in social settings. An extrovert prefers to live outside herself, as opposed to introversion where she prefers to be by herself. Most people are a mixture of the two, with greater tendencies toward one or the other.

## FEMINISM

Movement advocating political, social, and economic rights for women. Pursuit of equality for women with men in political, social, and economic status. Feminism seeks to understand gender inequality and the socially constructed roles of women in society. Today, feminism examines women's issues in a variety of cultures around the globe, including such problems as sexual harassment, domestic violence, and discrimination against women. Originally, the feminist movement dealt primarily with white women from industrialized nations. Charles Fourier (1792–1837), a French philosopher and writer, coined the term "feminism" in 1837.

## FETISH

A body part, such as a foot, or a practice that gives a person sexual desire; an erotic attachment to something; extreme devotion paid to an inanimate object; also something regarded with reverence and awe.

## FREUD, SIGMUND (1856–1939)

German psychologist and father of modern psychology and the founder of the psychoanalytic movement. By analyzing dreams and through studying free associations, Freud believed he could unlock the content of a person's unconscious mind to help resolve psychological conflicts. He developed many theories on human development and the structure of the mind; however, many of his ideas were hotly disputed and have been rejected by modern psychologists.

# FREUDIAN SLIP

A slip of the tongue, reflecting, in Freud's view, an unconscious impulse or desire. The unconscious mind contains emotions and memories of which we are not aware but that influence our thoughts, emotions, and behavior. Freud used the symbol of an iceberg to demonstrate the impact and size of the unconscious. Only the tip of an iceberg is visible, with the bulk hidden below the surface.

# GESTALT PSYCHOLOGY

In psychology, the theory that psychological and physiological events in the body occur based on a totality of experiences rather than on separate ones. Gestalt refers to how the mind, for instance, functions as a whole structure and that this whole has different properties than its individual parts. Founders of Gestalt therapy were Fritz Perls (1893–1970) and Laura Perls (1905–1990).

# *HOMO SAPIENS*

Humankind or modern humans; belonging to the species of primates that includes modern human beings. *Homo sapiens* are characterized by upright posture, language skills, and the use of tools, among other things. Modern humans are the only surviving member of the genus *Homo*.

# HYSTERIA

Extreme emotional reaction; a psychological disorder in which a person experiences violent emotional outbursts and irrational behavior. Sometimes a person experiencing hysteria can become physically paralyzed and unable to relieve himself of the hysterical state. Early psychologists such as Freud and Jean-Martin Charcot (1825–1893) were much occupied with trying to find a cure for hysteria.

# ID

One of the three parts of Freud's model of the mind. The id represents a person's disorganized, instinctual impulses, and if unchecked by the ego or superego, the id can lead to sociopathic behavior. Freud writes that in the id "contrary impulses exist side by side without canceling each other out." Freud regarded the id as the reservoir of the libido, the source of sexual impulses.

# INHIBITION

To restrain one's behavior; to refrain from acting in certain ways, either because of social constraints or because of memories of negative consequences, such as punishment or failure. Traumatic experiences often inhibit people from certain behaviors. Some consider inhibition to be a personality trait.

# INTELLIGENCE QUOTIENT

Also known as IQ. The score of a test designed to measure intelligence. It is determined by dividing mental age by a person's real age and then multiplying that number by 100. If a person scores 100, she is normal for her age (it's expected that 95 percent of the population will score between 70 and 135). IQ tests have somewhat fallen out of popularity since researchers now believe that other factors, including social skills, economic circumstances, and personality factors, also heavily determine a person's "intelligence."

# INTROSPECTION

Self-examination of one's emotions; looking inward for purpose and motivations; reflecting on one's life over a period of time. Introspection, discovering one's conscious and unconscious motivations, is critical to successful psychological analysis. Introspection is also important in philosophy as a means for discovering truth, as discussed by John Locke (1632–1704), David Hume (1711–1776), Thomas Hobbes (1588–1679), and others.

# INTROVERSION

Personality trait characterized by shyness and preference to be alone with oneself. The opposite of extroversion, which is the desire to be with people in high levels of social interaction. People may experience both states of mind in their lives, but many people swing sharply in one direction or another. Most models of personality development include scales of introversion to extroversion. Swiss psychologist Carl Jung is credited with first introducing these concepts.

# JINGOISM

Extreme devotion to country with a desire to wage war on other countries; also called belligerent nationalism. Jingoism also includes an irrational belief in the superiority of a person's country and its military and supports a foreign policy that encourages war and conquest of other nations to benefit one's own country.

# JUNG, CARL (1875–1961)

A Swiss psychotherapist who was a student of Sigmund Freud but broke away from Freud's psychoanalytic movement to form his own school of thought. Jung believed in individuation in which both the conscious and unconscious parts of people are integrated into a cohesive individual, although the conscious and unconscious work in their own ways. He also taught about extroversion and introversion as dimensions of personality and about archetypes as a key component of the unconscious mind.

# KANGAROO COURT

A self-appointed court that pretends to conduct a fair trial. Such a court is not official or duly elected and is entirely unfair and untrustworthy in its judgments. Although the term is almost always negative, there are a few cases where informal tribunals to settle issues have been called kangaroo courts.

## MALADJUSTMENT

In psychology, poor adjustment to psychological health and the meeting of life's social requirements or the stresses of daily living; emotionally unstable. A person who feels heightened anxiety in social situations is said to be maladjusted. A person may be said to be maladjusted if she fails to function fully in the interpersonal relationships of family, work, or school.

## MALTHUSIANISM

Teachings based on the ideas of Thomas R. Malthus (1766–1834). He believed that a population inevitably tends to increase faster than the food supply or means of subsistence. He theorized that the population grows at an exponential rate while the means of subsistence grow at an arithmetical rate. The result is always an inadequate supply of food and other necessities for life unless disease, war, or a natural disaster decreases the population. Malthus urged that sexual desires be repressed and reproduction of the human race limited.

## MANIA

A state of madness and sometimes violent behavior; extreme enthusiasm and impulsiveness beyond normal limits; a psychological disorder. The ancient Roman goddess of the dead was named Mania.

## MANIC DEPRESSION

Swings between strong feelings of happiness often accompanied by delusions and detachment from reality followed by depression and lassitude, then back to overenthusiasm and hyperactivity; a disorder characterized by extreme and deep mood swings and often called manic-depressive illness or bipolar disorder.

# MASOCHISM

Deriving satisfaction from suffering physical pain; a psychological disorder, wherein sexual satisfaction is derived from pain inflicted by another person. The term "sadomasochism" (combining both the pleasure from suffering pain and the pleasure derived from inflicting it) is taken from eighteenth-century French author the Marquis de Sade (1740–1814) whose novels depict cruel sexual practices.

# MATRIARCHY

A society governed by women; also refers to a situation in which a woman serves as the head of the family. In a matriarchal system, the right to rule descends from the female line of a family and the children of the family belong to the mother's clan. The male equivalent is patriarchy.

# MEGALOMANIA

In psychology, a condition in which a person has delusions that he is not who he really is. He believes that he possesses a greatness of character and personality and is obsessed with wealth and talents he does not have but believes himself to possess. Megalomania is commonly referred to as having "delusions of grandeur," but it can also refer to a lust for wealth, power, and recognition.

# MELANCHOLY

Feelings of mild depression or gloominess; sadness; emotional withdrawal and loneliness; or the inability to feel excitement or pleasure. In its severe form, melancholy can be diagnosed as clinical depression.

## MERITOCRACY

A society in which there exists a hierarchy based upon talent rather than wealth or privilege. A society in which people are rewarded based on the contributions they make. Meritocracy means the opposite of aristocracy, where wealth and privilege are handed down from family to family. The sociologist Michael Young coined the term in his 1958 book entitled *The Rise of the Meritocracy*.

## MISANTHROPE

A person who hates humanity or someone who dislikes people and sees the human race as misguided, selfish, and bothersome. A misanthrope keeps herself aloof from people.

## MISOGYNIST

Woman-hater; someone who hates and mistreats girls and women. The word derives from the Greek word *misogynes*, which literally means "woman-hater." Throughout history, women have been treated as second-class citizens. Relatively recently, in the first half of the twentieth century, women won the right to vote in the United States. In many countries, women have few rights.

## MORES

A culture's accepted values and customs. Mores are the way people are taught to behave based on the morals and values of their social group or society. Mores delineate how to behave in given social circumstances. What is right and proper in one social group may be considered wrong and improper in another culture. Mores are socially constructed.

# NARCISSISM

Extreme self-love or fascination with one's self image and/or mental abilities. Also a person considered egotistical and self-centered. Admiration of one's self to the exclusion of others around you. In psychology, Freudians believe that someone with a narcissistic personality remains at an infantile level of personality development. The world centers around the narcissist, just as an infant does not make an distinction between himself and the world around him.

# NATURALIZATION

The process by which a foreign-born person becomes a citizen. Nations have laws that allow people from other countries to reside within their borders as well as paths to citizenship for immigrants. Usually such applicants must demonstrate they will abide by the laws of the country and will be able to support themselves financially, as well as pass a test to show they have a basic understanding of the country's institutions, and customs.

# NATURE VS. NURTURE

Debate over how much an individual's personality is shaped by her environment or heredity and the degree to which she is genetically predisposed to certain traits and behaviors versus how much the nurture, love, experience, and values from her environment shape her. Today, most social scientists believe that both nature and nurture determine a person's personality, value-set, and dispositions. For example, genetic research shows a disposition toward alcoholism among certain families. However, living in an environment where alcohol consumption is discouraged can help overcome such a disposition. On the other hand, many studies involving identical twins, who share the same genes yet are raised apart, show striking similarities in likes and dislikes, career choices, and more.

# NEUROSIS

In psychology, a mild psychological disorder, resulting in anxiety and social maladjustment. A person who suffers from symptoms of neurosis is labeled a neurotic. A neurotic has difficulty regulating the levels of anxiety that build up as he engages in social situations he finds troubling. Sometimes a neurotic person will experience physical discomfort although there is nothing physically wrong.

# NUCLEAR FAMILY

In sociology, the term used to describe a family of two parents and at least one child living in the same household. Nuclear families are contrasted with nontraditional families, including single parents as well as multigenerational families living in the same household.

# OBSESSION

Excessive preoccupation with a single idea or set of ideas. Persistent ideas that are difficult to control, causing high levels of anxiety and stress. Obsession often distracts from productive endeavors. If not brought under control, it can result in obsessive-compulsive disorders, in which a person engages in compulsive behaviors in an effort to rid herself of the obsessions.

# PARANOIA

Extreme suspicion of people and organizations. In excessive amounts, paranoia can be classified as a mental disorder. Some psychologists believe that paranoia springs from unresolved personal conflicts. Over time, continuous feelings of paranoia can take their toll on an individual's personality.

# PARANOID SCHIZOPHRENIA

A condition in which a person suffers from illusions that seem real, causing great frustration and anxiety. A paranoid schizophrenic can experience delusions of grandeur as well as delusions of being followed and persecuted. Such delusions produce hallucinations.

# PARAPSYCHOLOGY

The study of supernatural phenomena, including extrasensory perception, clairvoyance, and the existence of ghosts and noncorporeal intelligences. Parapsychology deals with communications that seem to be beyond current human limitations.

# PATRIARCHY

A social system governed by men. The father is the supreme authority in the family, tribe, or clan. Patriarchy is the male equivalent to matriarchy. Feminists have been critical of the patriarchal structure of society, leading to the oppression of women. The word "patriarchy" originated in the 1630s.

# PECKING ORDER

One's place in the hierarchy of a family, company, or social group. The term was first used to describe the family hierarchy among breeds of poultry. Within a social group, often personality drives where a person places in the pecking order. Personality traits of introversion or extroversion can play a significant role in the maintenance and establishment of hierarchies.

# PEER GROUP

Group of people with characteristics in common, including social background, age, or education level. The peer group influences its members to think or act in a certain way. A person can belong to several peer groups based on where he lives, social circles, and employment.

## PETER PRINCIPLE

Facetious idea that in an organization every person will be promoted to the highest level of his or her incompetence. The idea comes from Dr. Lawrence J. Peter (1919–1990) and Raymond Hull (1919–1985) in their 1969 book *The Peter Principle*. The Peter Principle attempts to describe why so many companies, associations, and other organizations do foolish things.

## PHOBIA

Fear or strong aversion to a certain situation or thing. In stimulus-and-response theory, when the feared object is presented, the subject feels tremendous anxiety. There are many different kinds of phobias; for example, acrophobia is the fear of heights. Someone with acrophobia in an exposed high place experiences sweating, palpitations, and other physical symptoms of anxiety. People with phobias may understand intellectually that their fear is irrational, but this does not allay their symptoms.

## PLEASURE PRINCIPLE

In Freudian psychology, the instinct or drive for pleasure and avoidance of pain. Freud theorized that, of the three parts of a person's psyche, the id strongly desired pleasure unrestrained by any ethical or moral considerations. The super-ego, another of the three parts of a person's psyche, restrains pleasure-seeking activities. The ego balances the id and the superego.

## POSTINDUSTRIAL SOCIETY

A society in which the service sector produces more wealth than the industrial sector. Instead of manufactured products for sale domestically and globally being the leading factor in economic growth, a surge in the country's human capital of knowledge allows for providing services at a higher and higher rate. The shift to more science- and technology-related jobs and away from manufacturing or blue-collar jobs.

## PRIMOGENITURE

A system of inheritance based on the primacy of the first-born child (usually male). In the Middle Ages, the eldest son normally inherited. This system severely disadvantaged the younger sons, who often went into the church. Primogeniture is less common today. Postremogeniture is a custom by which the youngest son has rights to the family inheritance. Ultimogeniture gives the youngest son sole rights to the family estate to the exclusion of other brothers and relatives.

## PROJECTION

A defense mechanism whereby a person attributes his or her feelings or thoughts to other people's actions and motives. For example, blaming someone else for our failure is to project our failings onto that person rather than to take responsibility for our failure. Projection is a way of suppressing anxiety by expressing unconscious desires without consciously recognizing them.

## PSEUDOSCIENCE

Studies or theories claiming to be true science that fail to conform to the boundaries of science; a theory not supported by the scientific method of testing and observation, or a theory that lacks evidence to support its claims. People promoting pseudoscience will look at only the evidence that supports their claims and are skeptical of true scientific inquiry. Many consider such things as astrology and alchemy to be pseudoscience.

## PSYCHE

Originally in ancient Greece and Rome, the animating spirit. The term refers to the human mind and, by extension, the human soul or spirit. In psychology, the psyche is the mental or psychological structure of a person. Also known as the motivating force of a person or the center of emotion and consciousness.

# PSYCHOANALYSIS

In Freudian psychology, the process by which unconscious desires and wishes are brought to the surface where they can be analyzed and treated. Method of treating patients with mental disorders by revealing and interpreting unconscious desires discovered during dreams or through free association and hypnosis. Freud believed that people repress unconscious desires and that this repression causes mental disorders. He argued that solutions could be identified only by bringing the content of the unconscious to the surface.

# PSYCHOPATH

A person who exhibits antisocial behavior and a range of other symptoms. These can include shallow emotions, failure to establish friendships or loving family relationships, criminal behavior, egocentrism, and manipulation. Psychopaths can also be intelligent and charming, features that can add to the danger of this personality disorder.

# PSYCHOTHERAPY

Psychological treatment of mental disorders by a range of techniques. These include cognitive behavioral therapy, behavioral modification, group talk therapy, and more. Psychotherapy is designed to provide insights into causes of mental disorders and psychological maladjustments. The goal is to alleviate symptoms and help people grow as individuals so they can lead happier, more productive lives.

# REGRESSION

Reverting to an earlier stage of development. In psychology, the term means reverting back to a less-developed pattern of behavior or emotional well-being. For example, to defend against feeling anxiety about new responsibilities at work, a person may revert to immature behavior as if she were returning to adolescence, a time in her life when she had little responsibility. Freud classified regression as one of the defense mechanisms employed by people to protect their egos.

## RITE OF PASSAGE

The transitions in life from child to teenager to adult and into mature adult-hood. William Shakespeare (1564–1616) identified seven stages through which men and women pass: infancy, helpless; childhood, going to school; young adult, lover; soldier, fiery and hotheaded; the justice who has acquired wisdom; old age when a person loses his charm; and finally extreme old age, senility awaiting death.

## ROLE MODEL

A person who exhibits a specific behavior. In learning theory, a role model is a person who is respected and has credibility and, therefore, whose behavior is worthy of emulation. A role model can transmit values as well as help a person learn particular behaviors. Role models can have either positive or negative impacts on value judgments or overt behaviors.

## SADISM

Satisfaction in inflicting pain on another person; a psychological disorder in which sexual satisfaction is derived from causing pain to another person. The term is derived from eighteenth-century French author the Marquis de Sade whose novels depict cruel sexual practices.

## SCAPEGOAT

An innocent person or thing blamed for the wrongdoings of others. Having a scapegoat to blame eases people's consciences for wrongs they may have committed. The term comes from the biblical practice of the Hebrews of sym-bolically transferring the sins of the people onto a goat that is let loose in the wilderness to die.

# SENSORY DEPRIVATION

To cut off or gradually reduce a person's senses. Sensory-deprivation experiments demonstrate that people need sensory stimulation. A person who has experienced prolonged periods of sensory deprivation shows heightened anxiety levels, hallucinations, and depression. However, mild forms of sensory deprivation can relax people and be beneficial for those with high stress levels.

# SKINNER, B. F. (1904–1990)

A behavioral psychologist and researcher. He experimented with animals and people, studying how stimulus and response could lead to developing better learning behaviors. By presenting rewards and punishments, Skinner studied the responses of animals and people, observing how people react to different motivations to learn or perform various tasks. His school of psychology is known as radical behaviorism.

# SOCIALIZATION

To take on the social and cultural values, ideas, and traits of a family and larger social group. An infant learns about her environment through symbolic interactions with her mother and father, and other family members. Then as the child matures, she is further socialized by learning the cultural values and opinions of her neighborhood and school. Socialization helps people adapt to their environments so they can successfully live and function within their social construct.

# SUBCONSCIOUS

In psychology, the part of the unconscious mind that lies just beneath consciousness. According to Sigmund Freud, access to subconscious content was easier to obtain than to the deeper unconscious content of a person's mind. Freud used the symbol of an iceberg to demonstrate the three parts of the mind: Consciousness is above the surface of the water and represents only a small part of the mind. The subconscious is just below the surface, and the much larger portion of the iceberg represents the unconscious.

## SUBCULTURE

The culture and values of smaller groups within a larger society. Subcultures have their own set of attitudes, values, and behaviors. Subcultures may align along ethnic, economic, or social lines. They sometimes distinguish themselves from the mainstream culture through dress, hairstyles, or language.

## SUBLIMATION

In psychology, diverting mental energy of a biological impulse for pleasure into a more morally or socially acceptable use. Freud felt that people's natural impulses were sexual in nature. A sexually charged impulse, though, could be channeled, or sublimated, into a socially acceptable activity. Sublimation is one of Freud's defense mechanisms.

## SUBURBANIZATION

The process of urbanizing a rural area on the outskirts of a city; part of urban sprawl; to build communities spreading out from a heavily populated city where there is less crime and a slower pace of life. To accommodate the population explosion after World War II many suburbs sprang up, often close to manufacturing facilities.

## SUPEREGO

One of the three parts of Freud's psyche. The superego represents a person's desire to live an ethical, morally upright life. The other two parts of the mind are the id and the ego. The id represents a person's desires for pleasure, mostly sexual. The ego moderates between the id and the superego, maintaining a balance between the pleasure-seeking of the id and the moral imperatives of the superego.

# TOTEMISM

Belief among primitive tribal peoples that they are connected to some aspect of the natural environment, whether animate or inanimate. These natural objects include mountains, the sky, plants, and animals; they are called totems. Based on the totem from which a tribe creates its identity, the tribe develops rituals to help it celebrate and pass down its heritage to future generations.

# UNCONSCIOUS

A part of the mind that exists below the surface of conscious awareness. According to Sigmund Freud, the unconscious mind directs and influences our conscious decisions and actions. The unconscious contains memories, repressed feelings, and subliminal thoughts and ideas, as well as desires and fears. Freud believed that the human mind expressed the content of the unconscious in symbolic forms through dream symbols, slips of the tongue, and jokes—many a truth is told in jest, as the saying goes.

# VALUE JUDGMENT

A moral judgment as to whether something is right or wrong. A value judgment challenges a person to take an inventory of his moral system when evaluating decisions. Value judgments are different for different people because everyone has developed his or her own personal set of moral criteria.

# XENOPHOBIA

Fear or dislike of foreigners. Xenophobia is a product of both the cultural and language differences among people and of political and economic pressures. In the history of the United States, xenophobic attitudes have often developed as immigrants have come to America, threatening to take away jobs and opportunities from citizens. The Irish, Italians, and other nationalities have felt the effects of xenophobic attitudes.

# INDEX

Note: Page numbers in *italics* indicate main references.